WASHINGTON'S
UNDERSEA WAR

WASHINGTON'S UNDERSEA WAR

THE SECRET DEVELOPMENT OF THE SUBMARINE IN THE AMERICAN REVOLUTION

Shawn Shallow

gatekeeper press

All characters in the book are real. Their names, descriptions, and mannerisms were based on historical documents when obtainable. Given the secretive nature of the events, historical records of many activities were unavailable. As a result, some scenes and imagery were created to supplement historical accounts. Most dialogue has been adjusted for modern readability.

Published by Gatekeeper Press
3971 Hoover Rd. Suite 77
Columbus, OH 43123-2839

Layout Design by: Mr. Merwin D. Loquias

ISBN: 9781619844513
eISBN: 9781619844520

Printed in the United States of America

Thank you to David Aretha for editorial assistance.

CONTENTS

Dedicated to Margaret

CHAPTER 1
A DIFFICULT BEGINNING

He looked up at the clouds while taking in a long breath of the crisp air—pausing to contemplate the irony. He had taken breaths like these for granted, never thinking that they would soon be gone. He followed the clouds as they passed over a row of artillery leading to the tree to which his neck was tethered. His gaze then moved to nearby Dove Tavern, the source of merrymaking for many New Yorkers during happier times. Maybe its presence was a signal from the Almighty indicating that all was well and this terrible event would soon be over.

"Does the prisoner have any last words?" thundered the British officer almost to nobody in particular—more interested in making a spectacle for the onlookers.

Life had changed so quickly. He had seemed safe enough upon arrival posing as a schoolteacher looking for a faculty position. His cover story began to unravel almost immediately as people questioned why a young man from Yale would look for a teaching job so far from home, especially after the school year had already begun. Suspicion became heightened with his proximity to newly arrived British troops. An arrest quickly followed. Now, just twelve hours later, he was awaiting execution.

He cleared his throat and tried to remain composed as he recited the parting words rehearsed throughout the night. "I only regret that I have but one life to give for my country."

The end came quickly.

At his New Jersey field camp, George Washington sat dejected at his writing table. In this seated position, Washington's tall muscular frame and aristocratic bearing weren't clearly visible. However, his long chestnut brown hair, powdered for formal occasions, made a striking impression. Washington chose to wear his hair in a ponytail in a military style introduced by the Prussian Army and adopted by most European soldiers. It was believed that a man's hair pulled back tightly in this fashion made him look fierce. However, Washington's fair complexion and newly acquired reading glasses countered the effect.

Alexander Hamilton had just entered and delivered bad news. Typically Washington was glad to see his bright young artillery officer. He often marveled at how far Hamilton had come since his humble beginnings as an illegitimate orphan in the West Indies. Whoever the messenger, no man liked to learn that he had just sent a man to his death—especially when it involved an uncharacteristically reckless gamble on Washington's part.

It all started out promisingly enough in the summer of 1776. The British had evacuated Boston for parts unknown, leaving the city and New England to the rebelling Colonialists. But things quickly changed as the fleet reappeared to the south off the coast of Staten Island. This sighting confirmed Washington's fears that the British Navy saw the strategic importance of New York Harbor as a staging point for the British Army. From here, the British Army could thrust northward to join other forces moving south from Canada to encircle the Colonials in the middle. The end result would be a quarantine of the rebellious New England.

The British Army quickly landed on Staten Island unopposed with their Hessian mercenaries. They then attacked the Americans in New York City from two sides, forcing

Washington and his Colonials to retreat to Manhattan Island. In the end, General Washington retreated again, this time across the Harlem River, leaving New York to the British.

Now desperate for information to stave off further defeat, Washington attempted to gain intelligence any way he could. A volunteer emerged to seek this needed information in the form of a young Yale graduate, Nathan Hale.

Hamilton cleared his throat and began again. "A British officer came to our camp under a truce flag," he told Washington. "He relayed that Captain Hale had successfully passed through their army, both in Long Island and York Island, carrying sketches of the fortifications he had made of their number and different positions. However, Hale was apprehended before he could return and was brought before Sir William Howe. The sketches and notes found, concealed about his person, betrayed his intentions. When they found the papers, he declared his name, rank, and object for coming within the British lines."

Washington interjected feebly, "That immediate declaration should have been enough to secure a hearing, possibly leading to a prisoner exchange."

Hamilton paused, knowing that any concurrence would only elongate the painful narrative, and continued. "Sir William Howe gave orders for his execution the following morning. Before the execution, Captain Hale requested a clergyman but was refused by the provost marshal.

"He was refused a clergyman? That's outrageous," objected Washington.

"Yes, General. The British officer told me that the provost marshal in charge of Hale was a scaly man," affirmed Hamilton, using slang indicating a surly man of little character.

"A hooligan, I would say," grunted Washington.

After a pause, Hamilton continued. "The British officer went on to say that on the morning of his execution, his assigned station was near the fatal spot. The officer requested the provost marshal to permit Hale to sit in his marquee while the British mustered their company to witness the execution. He granted the request. The officer said that on entering the tent, Hale bore himself with gentle dignity in the consciousness of rectitude and high intentions. He asked for writing materials, which this officer furnished, whereupon Hale wrote two letters, one to his mother and one to a brother officer. He was shortly after summoned to the gallows. But a few persons were around him when he said his dying words: 'I only regret that I have but one life to give for my country.'"

At the end of the narrative, Washington sat silent for several minutes. Finally, he almost whispered, "And at twenty-one, what a short life it was." Washington rose and paced. "I should have never sent him. He didn't know the area to conceal the intent of his movements and create a meaningful excuse for his presence."

"I know his sacrifice is difficult to accept, but it was his to make. He volunteered knowing the risks," countered Hamilton in a vain attempt to relieve Washington's anguish.

"I appreciate your council, but we have many officers with zeal willing to take on disproportionate risk. It lies with me to give their efforts a good chance of success and select only those with the qualifications and a means to succeed."

After a moment, Hamilton cautiously continued. "Nevertheless, General, we need to gather intelligence on the enemy's strength and movements to have any chance of defense. Is there anyone with the contacts to gather this information? We have some funds to compensate the noncombatants for their risk."

Washington sat once again in quiet contemplation before continuing. "It's a difficult order to fill. Honor and risk seem to be at odds with the desire for compensation," said Washington, referring to the unnatural coexistence of spying and warfare. Spies were normally seen as traitors, happy to sell their secrets for a price, in contrast to the code of honor shared by most soldiers. However, the normal rules seemed warped in the American Colonies. Tories, loyal to the English, coexisted with Patriots, who considered the British hostile occupiers. Both sides were eager to pass information without a need for lucrative compensation.

"I believe the lack of honor the grenadiers have demonstrated has inclined a number of colonists to be sympathetic to our cause," muttered Hamilton with restrained disgust. During the occupation of Boston, assaults by British troops among local women by individuals or groups were commonplace. Complaints to the British command and municipal authorities fell on deaf ears. It was clear that the colonists were treated as the population of a conquered land and therefore the spoils of war. Many colonists naturally responded by seeing themselves as the British saw them, no longer British subjects due the rights and privileges of the empire.

"Yes, the ungentlemanly behavior will certainly continue and even become more extreme in New York and Long Island. I need to change my thinking," affirmed Washington. "I will carefully consider a plan. Unlike before, I must have the patience and discipline to find the right man with the mindset and disposition to carefully build a small network of trusted confidants."

Hamilton reached for his short green coat, signifying his position in the New York Forrester Regiment. Uniform variations were a continuous problem for Washington, who preferred a standard for increased discipline.

"Timely and secure delivery of the information will be a problem," countered Hamilton, now moving to leave. Careful movement of meticulously concealed and often encrypted information took time and delivery coordination they just didn't have.

"Yes," continued Washington, now lost in thought, "it will take a special man to fit such a shopkeeper's order."

CHAPTER 2
STRANGE LITTLE MAN

Not far away, David Bushnell walked the tiny campus of Yale College. As usual, he drew a few glances from those noting his departure from a typical student. The other colligates came from well-to-do families representing the aristocracy of the colonies. Most were the children of doctors, lawyers, and successful merchants—typically entering Yale at just fifteen. David, on the other hand, was the son of a farmer and nearly thirty-three. Unlike a farmer, David was small and slight with the look of a clerk rather than a powerful man who worked the earth.

David's late entrance to college couldn't be helped. He had expected to remain a farmer like his brother Ezra despite having no skill for it. But his fortune changed almost four years earlier when his father passed away. David quickly sold his interest in the family farm to his brother with the intention of using the proceeds to finance an education. But first, there were obstacles to overcome. To begin with, as was typical for a Colonial farmer, David had only the most rudimentary of educations spanning less than three years—not nearly enough to apply for college. For lack of a better idea, David turned to the most learned man he knew, the Reverend John Devotion, his hometown minister in Saybrook, Connecticut. Luckily, the reverend knew David as an upstanding man and agreed to spend the next two years teaching him what would normally be conveyed in ten for a member of the Colonial elite. David's brilliant mind quickly absorbed all that the reverend knew and easily entered Yale at the advanced age of thirty—no small feat for a man of such little education and family standing.

Initially, David sat in the small classrooms feeling inadequate because of his age and poverty. The other boys spoke with eloquence and confidence from having pristine educations. But David quickly moved ahead as he easily grasped new advancements from the fields of mathematics and the natural philosophies (later known as science). David reveled in the works of Isaac Newton, who not that many years earlier had determined that light was made of small particles. Joseph Priestly made similar discoveries with air. But, most of all, he scrutinized the work of colonist Benjamin Franklin, whose recent discoveries in electricity had shocked the world.

David quickly become absorbed in reading anything and everything in the Yale Library. He was particularly fond of a publication entitled, *English Gentleman's Magazine*, which featured articles of interest for "men of higher learning," including theories about the natural philosophies.

Starting from the beginning, David had progressed to a volume published just twenty-five years earlier containing a rudimentary sketch that would change his life. David read with curiosity how a Danish scientist, Cornelius Drebbel, theorized how an air-filled tank could be built to descend below the water and rise again. The drawing was simple. Add water to descend and expel water to rise. In this way, a large container could go to the bottom of a body of water. David began to ponder the possibilities and theorized more advanced variations of his own, which he finally produced for his close friend Phineas in the Yale Library.

"Explain this object," said Phineas, pointing to a corkscrew-like device at the top and side of the water machine in David's roughly sketched schematic. His idea would later be called a propeller.

"It's like a windmill. It pushes water, just like air moves the shaft. Only it works backwards. I figure that if you move the shaft, it will move the water."

Phineas had to think for a second. "That makes sense. What about this thing?" he asked, pointing again.

"These two brass tubes conduct air when you need it. The one on top takes in the air; the one next to it removes the bad air." Future generations would call it a snorkel.

"What is this thing at the bottom?"

"It's a tube that lets in water for ballast."

"I thought this was for ballast," said Phineas, pointing to weights.

"That's ballast too, but that is more for staying underwater once you have completed your descent. This tube allows the machine to raise and lower in the water. You know, to reach equilibrium." This would later be called a ballast pump.

Phineas pondered the drawing. He knew David to be intelligent beyond anyone's comprehension, but this seemed too fantastic. However, these were wondrous times in a volatile world.

No place was more volatile than the American Colonies. Many colonists were starving as the massive British fleet routinely intercepted American ships trying to import food to besieged New York. If left unchecked, the Americas would slowly dwindle as the economy stagnated. The only way to help the colonies was to find a way to deal with the British fleet.

David broke the silence. "The more I thought about Dremel's tank, the more I saw the possibilities."

"You mean to break the blockade?" whispered Phineas, who just realized that this was not just a theoretical exercise.

"Yes, I know it seems fantastic, but the logic is quite simple. Maritime strategists tell us that there are basically two ways to defend against enemy ships. You can either destroy their means to maneuver with cannon fire to their masts or rudder or burn them with a fireship. Either way, you have to approach them with a superior ship and survive the withering gunfire. The only other means is to approach in the secrecy of darkness. With no fleet, we must endeavor to do that."

"Even at night a ship would be seen eventually in an open harbor," continued Phineas. "So, you think that approaching underwater is the answer?"

"Yes," affirmed David sheepishly as if hearing it out loud made it sound absurd.

"But even if you could get there, you would have to come to the surface to be seen and launch some sort of bomb. Everyone knows that you cannot explode gunpowder underwater," objected Phineas. The two were now hunched together, speaking in the lowest possible tones.

"I know that's the theory," countered David, "but what if you could encapsulate gunpowder, air, and the fuse in some sort of separate container and attach it to the ship. Then all you need is some delayed devise to trigger a spark inside the container."

Phineas leaned back. He didn't know if David was another Leonardo da Vinci or just insane. Either way, there was little future in it. However, David was his friend and he was reaching out to him for help.

"I suppose the first step is to see if you really can explode gunpowder underwater. Everything else is unnecessary if you cannot inflict damage on a ship," observed Phineas.

A student walked by, causing a pause in the conversation. After he glanced suspiciously at the two whispering conspirators, they cautiously continued.

"How can I do it without rousting the authorities?" asked David. Phineas knew David well. He might be a genius, but a timid genius, always afraid—for good reason.

Phineas paused for a moment. "If you keep the rest secret, exploding gunpowder underwater would not arouse suspicion—especially if you do it in the open at Yale. It will be seen as just another experiment."

David was instantly wary of such a plan. It seemed counterintuitive to do it in the open. The consequences of being seen as developing a weapon to assist the Patriots would be severe. He would have to carefully consider the risk—to himself and his family back home.

CHAPTER 3
WASHINGTON'S NEW PLAN

Benjamin Tallmadge stood before Washington in his field tent wearing the more customary blue waistcoat of a Colonial regular. While Washington preferred that the Army adopt the loose brown Virginia hunting shirt with pockets as the standard, he bowed to the Continental Congress' desire for style. In the end, he ordered most soldiers to provide themselves with a coat of blue and red to distinguish from the British redcoats.

Tallmadge, at just twenty-four, wore his hair slightly shorter than Washington. His lanky frame was punctuated by keen eyes reflecting his extreme intellect. Tallmadge had personally vouched for his college associate, Nathan Hale, in a letter to the general securing him an officer's commission. As a result, Tallmadge had taken the news of Hale's execution hard. Nevertheless, Washington's summoning was a mystery. The general was not known to express condolences for men lost in the line of duty.

"Mr. Tallmadge, I understand that you hail from Long Island," said Washington, more as a tactical question to a line officer than a friendly inquiry.

"Yes, General. My father was a clergyman in Setauket outside the township of Brookhaven," affirmed the major.

Washington paused a moment before continuing. "I find your work to be thorough and consistent in approach, but not impulsively aggressive."

Tallmadge knew that Washington was desperate for any victory against the British, and this conversation was not going in the direction he might have hoped.

"Yes, General," affirmed Tallmadge. "I am careful. However, I can certainly profit from any instruction your excellency cares to impart."

Washington softened his voice and changed tack. "Major, I'm deeply sorry about how Mr. Hale met his death. I bear full responsibility for his sacrifice. He went on the mission without foreknowledge of the territory, the people, and without an adequate disguise. I endeavor to lead no more young men to such a fate as his."

Tallmadge looked down. "I know that he knew the risks, General. But his death will likewise haunt me all my days."

Washington continued to sit in gloomy quiet for a moment, and then rose.

"I have given the situation much thought. Local men must be our sojourners for information—gathered from among their closest friends and family. Secrecy will be our weapon of necessity."

Tallmadge stood eye to eye with his superior in an uncomfortable stare.

"I am your servant, General."

After another pause, Washington withdrew toward a writing table. "Please sit and we will work."

As Tallmadge moved to sit, Washington peered at his map of Long Island and New York Harbor. "You better than anyone know that General Howe now occupies Long Island and New York. That is where your brother is, I believe."

Benjamin and his brother William had enlisted at the same time. Unfortunately, William was captured and delivered to a prison ship, where men were left to starve. Benjamin and his family attempted to deliver food and blankets through multiple channels, to no avail. Finally, William died of depravation and was discarded over the side. It was a terrible blow to Tallmadge, who lost both Nathan Hale and his brother to British jailers.

"Yes, General" was all Tallmadge could say. It was better to leave Washington in the dark than open those wounds again.

Washington continued. "Unfortunately, we are unable due to our proximity to lessen the burden on our brethren or gain insight into the enemy's activities ourselves. We have little information on the state of our enemy's forces and need to gain knowledge of their troop movements and supplies. With this in hand, we can develop a clear strategy of our own."

"Yes, General," confirmed Tallmadge. "Only a local resident sympathetic to our cause would be able to gather this information in the course of their daily life without suspicion."

Now Washington paused with a sigh. "That is precisely the reason I unwittingly sacrificed the life of a fine young officer. He attempted to gather information without the benefit of knowing how to avoid suspicion or evade detection."

Tallmadge knew of the execution in great detail, as did every soldier. However, he made no sign of affirmation; he just sat silent.

"So," continued Washington, "if you have a mind to undertake this important work, I was earnestly hoping you would devote your energy to developing a means of gathering this information from local associates of your intimate trust without undue risk to them or yourself. Perhaps even more difficult, I need this information delivered in plain sight of the Philistines themselves with extreme haste and no cloud of suspicion."

Tallmadge reflected on Washington's words. This was a huge undertaking involving the greatest risks regardless of the precautions. The task seemed monumental.

Sensing his trepidation, Washington continued more slowly. "I understand, Benjamin, that this is no easy task to be completed in a fortnight. It will take many weeks of careful contemplation, quiet inquiries, and time to develop. I myself was involved in a similar effort but a fraction of this size in the French and Indian Wars."

Washington, while in his early twenties, had volunteered to gather intelligence by intermingling with French soldiers. His lifelong avoidance of alcohol proved to his advantage as he gathered information from party-going soldiers while keeping his wits about him. Tallmadge, like most Americans, was familiar with Washington's role in gathering the information. It came to comprise a small part of the larger-than-life Washington legend in the Americas.

Washington continued. "It is because of this small experience that I understand the importance and difficulty of the assignment I am placing before you. I likewise know that you are the only man that has the skills and countenance to accomplish such a task."

Tallmadge sat silent. He, in fact, felt he had neither the skills nor the countenance. But he also knew firsthand what was at stake.

After more discussion, Tallmadge took his leave. As he surveyed the sky, he wondered if a similar scene greeted Nathan Hale as the rope was placed around his neck. Hopefully his efforts would not come to that.

CHAPTER 4
THE EXPERIMENT

David waded into the pond within view of a handful of onlooking students. Just as Phineas had predicted, the gunpowder experiment was seen as a purely academic pursuit. As a result, some students were on hand to watch the peculiar little man in hopes of witnessing a colorful failure for the day's entertainment.

Phineas looked on as David waded into chest-high water. Stopping in the center of the pond, David took a wooden bottle and carefully submerged it to the bottom with a tube attached. To keep the device upright, he pushed the bottle slightly into the murky sediment. As the onlookers strained to see his next move, David lit the end of the tube with a flame and carefully waded to the side trying not to disturb the bottle below. He then jumped a few feet to where Phineas was crouching to watch. Nothing happened for what seemed like an eternity. It must be as everyone predicted; you can't explode gunpowder under water.

Chuckles, followed by open laughter, greeted David from the youthful onlookers. Then as they were turning to depart, a loud explosion rocked the area, covering all spectators with pond water. Students and teachers alike came running to see the source of the noise. He had done it.

Because the experiment was contrary to current theories of combustion and water, David was asked several weeks later by the faculty to replicate the effort. An ensuing crowd surrounded the pond in lines two people deep.

"I can't believe how many people are here," whispered David nervously.

"Don't worry," assured Phineas. "They're all with Yale College. There's no Tories about to cause trouble."

"What about the headmaster? Are we sure of his affiliations?" asked David, glancing at the school's president who surprised everyone by attending the event in person.

"We can't worry about that right now. We have to get the experiment going. The crowd is getting restless."

The second (experiment) was with two pounds of gunpowder, enclosed in a wooden bottle and fixed under a hogshead, with a two inch oak plank [the customary thickness of an oceangoing ship's hull] between the hogshead and the powder. The hogshead was loaded with stones as deep as it could swim [descend naturally]. The tube descending through the top of the hogshead and through the plank into the powder contained in the bottle was primed with powder. A match put to the priming exploded the powder with very great effect, rending the plank into pieces, demolishing the hogshead and casting the stones, ruins of the hogshead, and a body of water many feet into the air, to the astonishment of the spectators.

–Excerpt from a letter sent years later by David, 1787, to an inquisitive Thomas Jefferson

The professors witnessing the explosion were dumbfounded. The dream of an underwater weapon going back eleven hundred years to Alexander the Great was realized, and it was a student who did it.

CHAPTER 5
FIRST SPY RECRUIT

Benjamin Tallmadge approached the Black Bonnet tavern. It was just a short month since he had been with Washington to discuss creation of the spy ring. From the tavern's exterior, he could hear the drunken merriment of what was obviously a group of soldiers. For a moment, he thought about making a hasty retreat. But his hesitation caught the attention of two onlookers. Leaving now would signal his aversion to the king's men. If detained on suspicion, the risk of being identified as a Colonial regular out of uniform would be literally fatal. As casually as he could, Tallmadge entered the tavern and approached the publican behind the rough semblance of a bar and quietly ordered stout ale.

The soldiers seemed to take no notice of the man and continued to make merriment. It seemed that the object of their entertainment was one soldier describing a "grab" he had recently done to a Colonial home. A "grab" was soldier slang referring to stealing the homeowner's possessions while he was still in the house. In this case, based on the soldier's description of the owner's terrified look, he was in the same room as his looters. Most of the other soldiers sat incredulous, most of their stealing limited to "lobbing" or robbery while the owner was away.

After a time, a nondescript man of thirty, but acting almost elderly by his timid movements, entered in the form of Abraham

Woodhull. Tallmadge quietly rose and greeted his childhood friend with a handshake and subdued clap on the back, lest they gather any more attention. Even if there were no soldiers present, Tallmadge would have done the same knowing the character of his sedate friend.

The bartender seemed tense and nervously glanced at the soldiers. Could it be that he suspected the two strangers as being Patriots? Tallmadge placed two guineas on the bar as if to show he would be well compensated for their presence. He then turned his attention to his old friend.

"How are you? I hear that your business is doing well."

Tallmadge saw a glimpse of a woman brush behind the curtain. Could it be that the barman was not anxious about his presence, but of the British soldiers who were notorious for the sexual assault of Colonial women?

It appeared that one of the soldiers saw her too and approached the bar. Sensing potential danger for the woman, Tallmadge rose to intercept.

"May I buy a flip for a fine British soldier?" asked Tallmadge, referring to a small ale.

The man wearing the characteristic coat of red and the black cocked hat of the British Cold Stream Guards was taken off guard. Like the Continental Army, the British had some uniform variations of their own.

"I believe you are a Cold Stream Guard if I'm not mistaken," continued Tallmadge, pointing to his telltale hat known to most.

"Aye, that I am," he cautiously responded.

"I was about to salute good King George with my friend and we'd be honored to share it with a king's man."

Now the soldier had little choice and grudgingly accepted the drink. After bringing the libations, Tallmadge glanced at the barman to signal an instruction to remove the potential victim of the assault. He gladly obliged by slipping behind the curtain to usher her out.

"Here's to King George. May he have a long and happy reign."

After taking the drink, the soldier grudgingly returned to his merrymaking friends. Tallmadge and Woodhull sat quietly for a moment before returning to their discussion.

Their conversation came naturally. Tallmadge and Woodhull had been neighbors growing up. When the troubles came, Tallmadge was eager to join the Continental Army, while Woodhull was satisfied to maintain the quiet life of a civilian bachelor. They were likewise different in every other respect. Tallmadge excelled in academics, being fluent in Greek and Latin, while Woodhull quietly wandered the forest enjoying the outdoors in quiet solitude. Woodhull's only affection for the company of people was time spent with his two older sisters, one of whom owned a boardinghouse in Manhattan. His quiet life would have continued had it not been for the death of his two older brothers. As a result, Woodhull was forced to assume the role as patriarch, managing the family's land holdings and business interests. As such, he traveled frequently to and from his sister's home in Manhattan.

It was this rare combination of quiet reservation with routine business travel to the heart of enemy territory that made him such a valuable commodity. Add the fact that his sister's boardinghouse often contained Tories in conversation about British movements and you had the perfect combination.

"So, that's the plan," said Tallmadge, ending his narrative. "Obviously, in addition to being a center for British military activity, it's also the center of all social activities for officers—perfect for collection of errant slips of the tongue."

Woodhull sat quietly for a moment, then cautiously interjected. "You're sure that my name will be known by no one? Obviously, I have my family and sisters to think about."

"Absolutely," interjected Tallmadge. "Only George Washington and myself will know your name. All information will be transported by a courier at a prearranged drop point."

"And the messages will be undetectable if intercepted?"

With this Tallmadge paused. "We will have to be very careful in our use of code and how the information is conveyed in normal-looking documents like shipping manifests. We can use satchels of goods for delivery and whatever other means would be seen as normal for a merchant. However, I won't lie to you. Any slip-ups could mean our lives. We will have to be especially careful not only of our documents, but also the manner and frequency of the courier."

"How do you suggest obtaining a courier?"

"Well, I thought you would be in the best position of selecting a trusted friend that already travels the areas between your normal route and the remaining distance to our contact," said Tallmadge, now bringing Woodhull that much deeper into the plot. "It's important that they are a normal fixture of the environment. Their movements cannot arouse suspicion."

Tallmadge mused over the proposition. "I normally travel on the Brooklyn ferry. After that, I would need a man to transport the information the rest of the way, primarily over water."

"Do you know such a man?" asked Tallmadge.

"I do know such a man. A stout-hearted one at that," mused Woodhull.

It appeared that the spy network had its first recruit and a second in its sites.

CHAPTER 6
THE FAMILY BUSINESS

D avid walked up the country lane to the family farm. It seemed almost like a dream approaching the barn and adjacent log-hewn cabin that had been his home for so long. So much had happened in the three years since his departure for Yale that it seemed like a lifetime ago.

Most farms in the area were fairly well-to-do. Prominent farmers shipped tons of corn, wheat, and rice to the West Indies and Europe. However, the Bushnell family farm tended toward those found nearer the "backcountry." These farms, typically found further inland, were smaller and often managed by younger sons who did not inherit the family holdings of eldest brothers. A powerful man, the opposite of David in almost every way, appeared from the little shed.

"David," blurted the startled Ezra.

"Hello, brother."

David and Ezra were close from an early age. The larger and more powerful Ezra became the protector of his smaller sibling. David's peculiar mannerism, inherent with a child genius, made him doubly the target of bullying. He was well known for being lost in thought and unaware of the activities going on around him-making him an easy target for pranks. As a result, they developed a special bond. David trusted Ezra implicitly for his strength and devotion. Ezra trusted David's intellect, which had proven infallible.

"What brings you back from Yale College? Have you trouble with the other lads?" asked Ezra with the natural reflex of coming to his aid.

"No, Ezra. I came because I need help with an invention."

Ezra grinned. It was like old times. David would devise some contraption and Ezra would use his natural dexterity to try it out. Early on, the effort often turned into having their ears boxed by their father, who was intent on having them focus instead on never-ending chores.

"I should have known. What is it then, a new wagon that pulls itself?"

David just peered at Ezra, processing the question. He was devoid of virtually all humor, even the practiced humor of his brother.

"No," countered David after a moment. "It's an underwater wagon that *you* propel."

Now it was Ezra's turn to be dumbfounded. He knew from long experience that David was totally sincere at answering the question put to him.

"Come inside and tell me all about it over supper," said Ezra, gesturing to the cabin.

After Ezra and David consumed steaming bowls of pottage, or thick soup, they began to catch up.

"What news do we have of the war?" asked Ezra.

"I understand that the British control New York Harbor. The Patriots control the rivers including the Hudson. General Howe has a small garrison near Trenton, Princeton, and Bordertown, but the majority of his Army remains in New York."

"Well, we still have West Point," interjected Ezra. West Point sat astride the Hudson River at a critical point where it made two ninety-degree turns. The first turn was to the west at Martelaer's Rock, and the second was to the north between Butter Mountain and Breakneck Ridge. Approaching ships and smaller river craft had to slow down to make numerous changes in tack. These changes in sail position were made more harrowing by shifting winds in the narrow river gorge. The end result was vulnerability to enemy fire, which the Patriot-controlled West Point was happy to provide.

"Yes," affirmed David, "but their control of New York Harbor is choking the city."

Ezra knew all too well. Farmers couldn't bring their goods to area residents without being accosted by the British, who needed food for their huge army. That meant most of their harvest was confiscated. As a result, farmers were left without northern markets and had to ply their goods to the south in far-away Philadelphia and other cities. New York and Boston were cut off.

There was a long silence as they both enjoyed their soup. Finishing and moving that much closer to the fire, David introduced the reason for his visit.

"I mean to break the blockade, Ezra."

Ezra was normally quick to join his brother in whatever his mind conjured. But this seemed too risky even for him.

"How can you break the blockade with the underwater wagon? I thought you were making a joke," responded Ezra without any malice in his voice, just an honest inquiry.

"Yes, with the underwater wagon. I've made a drawing, you see," said David, now fumbling with papers contained in a satchel.

This was not the first drawing of inventions Ezra had examined, but these were certainly the most unusual. David proceeded to walk through each component and their operation. In the end, Ezra sat in silence, only the dancing light from the fire changing his features.

"You want me to help you build it, then pilot it from under the ocean," said Ezra finally, with a hint of quiet desperation in his voice.

David sat back in his wooden chair. It obviously seemed too fantastic even to Ezra.

CHAPTER 7
SECOND SPY RECRUIT

In a dark inlet, Woodhull, Tallmadge's first spy recruit, squinted to see through the darkness enveloping the water. Normally he would have expected to see a small oil lamp on the dock to guide approaching sloops at such an hour. But clandestine activity called for discretion, as pointed out by Tallmadge during their lengthy planning session. Finally, a barge silently crept to the dock.

Almost on cue, two men appeared from the shadows to take the mooring lines. Each glanced nervously at Woodhull at the far end of the dock. As the bargemen hauled in the lines, the barge captain, Caleb Brewster, perceived the discomfort and indicated to his men to quietly retreat.

"Who be you there?" challenged a wary Brewster, perched behind the gunwale.

"You don't recognize your old friend?" responded Woodhull, approaching the barge.

Looking closer, Brewster smiled and gave a muffled laugh. Turning on his heel he gave a nod to his crew. "Go about your business, lads. I'll talk a few moments with this gent." Grabbing the foremast shroud, Brewster swung his body ashore with a movement as natural as any man walking.

"What brings a respectable merchant to see a group of ne're-do-wells in the dark of night?"

"Can't an old friend just be about for an evening stroll?" chided Woodhull.

"Not here. You'd do well to keep your day's wages hidden in your pocket and your skull in one piece. Or, worse yet, become the guest of a king's warship for two years." Brewster was referring to the British practice of "pressing" men into naval service—usually with a billy club in the back of the head.

"True enough. Dangerous place for both of us to be caught. You by a press gang and me as a Patriot sutler," confirmed Woodhull, referring to himself as a merchant who supplied Washington's army.

"Aye, what the British patrols wouldn't give to get their hands on me and my mates. But not for seamanship." Brewster was referring to the smuggling trade, which was alive and well in the colonies. That was also part and parcel of what merchants went through to supply Washington. But even in the prewar years, taxes and corrupt customs officials made honest business impossible. Even if a seagoing merchant could afford the tariffs levied on his cargo, the British Navy more often than not confiscated what they wanted without compensation.

"That's why I'm here. I need you to quietly carry something of importance. It's different than your typical cargo."

"People then?" asked Brewster with a wary glance.

"Sometimes, but more often just a parcel with letters that seem to discuss mundane family news. Or, sometimes a normal book with something in the bindings."

"So, it's information you want passed for the Patriots. That's the most dangerous of all," said Brewster with a wrinkled frown.

Woodhull paused for a moment to acknowledge that his friend's observation was true. "Yes. You are absolutely correct. Some will be gathered by a friend in New York. Some will come from Long Island." Woodhull paused, then looked intently at his friend. "And some will come from you. There is nobody better than yourself when it comes to knowing the comings of Long Island Sound and the harbor."

Brewster stood silent, then proceeded cautiously. "Aye. I know better than most the comings and goings around here and I can guard the parcels. But, I don't know your friends." Brewster was making reference to a sad situation enveloping the coastal areas. Tories loyal to the king often passed as Patriots to avoid the wrath of more patriotic-minded neighbors. The Patriots likewise posed as Loyalist Tories to avoid arrest. In the end, it was impossible to know friend from foe.

"That's the beauty of the plan. My friends are even more wary of discovery than you because they are not so able to slip into the night. They will not know who you are, or you they. In fact, I won't even know all participants should I be interrogated by the British. One contact will send you a signal of your own design to know when a parcel requires delivery. They will never see you face to face."

"So, how will they know that the parcel is safe until my retrieval?"

"They won't. That's why the information contained in the parcel will be made to appear so ordinary."

"Sounds clever enough," said Brewster finally.

"There will be some payment for you and your men, but not enough to cover your risk. You have to do it for your own reasons," said Woodhull with sincerity.

"Oh, we have reason enough," growled Brewster. More than anyone else, he saw the injustices performed by so-called British gentlemen officers.

After they conversed for a few more minutes, Woodhull turned to go.

"I'll find you again in a fortnight or thereabouts."

Tipping his hat, Woodhull turned toward the deserted dock. One down and two more to go.

CHAPTER 8
THE HIDING PLACE

David stared into the black ocean, softened only by the eerie fog caressing its surface. A ghostly silence blanketed the water, interrupted by the quiet creeks and lapping of his rowboat's oars.

"The island looks bedeviled, as usual," interjected Ezra, now peering landward.

After the initial shock had worn off, Ezra and David spent two days working out how and where they could build the underwater wagon without rousting the British. The final conclusion was obvious—an unused fishing shack of their acquaintance at the mysterious Poverty Island.

David looked up to see the island's shoreline emerging through the mist. It appeared that Ezra's mood was not unlike David's.

"Remember what Granddad said?" inquired David. Ezra nodded.

There were many legends surrounding the "haunted island." Some involved ghouls, demons, dead Indians, and even ghostly specters lost at sea. But the most well-known legend was that of Lady Fenwick, who was said to haunt the small pile of land as a witch. Stories of witches and demons were common in the colonies. Some came from the old country while some started in the new world. David's grandfather told them about some of the troubles that had happened in the nearby Massachusetts Colony when he was only twelve. In the end, over 150 people had been imprisoned or executed by the people of Salem for supposed demonic activity. It was this event that caused their grandfather to teach them a valuable lesson. To make sure the boys understood, he firmly planted his hands on his hips and said, "Boys, always remember that people are much more dangerous than ghosts."

So they pressed through the morning fog to finally make the island. It was filled with underbrush and definitely uninhabited by people. David lurched forward as the boat ran up onto a small sandy beach in front of their fishing shack. They'd purchased the shack from a fishing club that had abandoned it earlier as a place to work on their water machine. With British informants about, they needed a safe and secluded place to work, unseen by prying eyes. What better place than under the guise of fishing on an island reputed to be haunted. They sat silently in their boat as was their custom, trying to hear any unwanted Colonials, or even British soldiers. Luckily, the silence remained pristine.

"We will hide our wood there," said David, pointing to an area near the water but hidden by the shack. Trees and wood were plentiful in the colonies. Tanners used tree bark in the leather-curing process. Potash from burned trees was used by soap makers and glassblowers, among others. More importantly, wood was easily shaped for everything from boats to barrels, with pitch applied for waterproofing joints. Given the widespread demand for wood, local sawmills were plentiful and easily accessed for building materials. So, there was no need to cut their own. However, David and Ezra would have to transport it to the island without being intercepted by the ever-present in-shore squadron.

"How many trips do you think we'll have to make to bring the wood?" asked David.

Ezra contemplated the question. "At least three, I think. We can't bring too much or we'll be slowed down and the target of many questions."

"Can we start tomorrow?" asked David, wide-eyed as if they were teenagers again?

"Yes," affirmed Ezra with a little less enthusiasm. "We just have to get the in-shore squadron to cooperate."

CHAPTER 9
THIRD SPY RECRUIT

"So that's the plan," summarized Woodhull. "Your tavern will be the transfer point."

Austin Roe, the would-be third spy recruit, sat silent. His situation made him the unlikeliest candidate to be a spy for Washington. Unlike Brewster, who could slip into the darkness of the waterfront, Roe had a business and family to protect. Even more, he had a tavern. That meant he was always in the public eye and subject to the whims of his customers. If there was even a whiff of doubt about his affection for the Crown, his Loyalist patronage would stop drinking and eating at his business. Worse yet, they could easily destroy the business and have him thrown into prison with his family.

"You're sure that nobody will know my name?" Roe quizzed again.

"Absolutely not," Woodhull replied. "We each will have a code name and false occupation as a cover story.'"

"And the system has been developed to avoid suspicion?"

"Yes. I will collect information in New York while visiting my sister's boardinghouse. I've been there regularly for years and have become part of the local scenery. I will deliver the information to your tavern myself."

"What if you appear too regularly?" countered a cautious Roe.

"I will drop off the information in a field behind the tavern at a prearranged spot under the cover of darkness. You can retrieve the information at such a time as you deem safe."

A long silence ensued as Roe absorbed the enormity of the request. "I suppose it won't hurt to be seen together." Roe's family had known the Woodhulls for years. In fact, his father had purchased what would become the tavern from Woodhull's father. So, being seen together would not seem out of place.

A pub regular approached the counter a few feet down and addressed Roe. "Might I trouble you for a trencher of pap?"

In response, Roe absentmindedly left the conversation to enter the back room and emerged with a wooden plate of cornmeal pudding. Since it took hours to cook, he typically started it the night before and left it over the fire all the next day for meals. After receiving his food, the patron retreated to a nearby table.

Woodhull began again. "I was hoping that on occasion you could gather information yourself here or in New York when you purchase supplies."

"I suppose," said Roe pensively. "I do hear a lot from my patrons over a pint and those lobsterbacks on occasion. And, of course, I do travel to New York for supplies."

"Either way," continued Woodhull. "We signal to the courier that a package is ready for delivery to General Washington." Caleb Brewster and his barge were literally a stone's throw away from the tavern. Brewster would take the package by boat across the sound and deliver it right to Major Tallmadge.

"How long will it take to complete the full trip?" asked a skeptical Roe.

"I reckon about two weeks," said Woodhull with a frown.

"That is a long time for information on troop movements and such," countered Roe.

"I don't know of any faster way without arousing suspicions," said Woodhull firmly, as if he had had this conversation before with Major Tallmadge. The tone reaffirmed Roe.

After discussing a few more details and concerns, they concluded their business with a handshake. Just days later, the process would begin.

CHAPTER 10
THE IN-SHORE SQUADRON

David and Ezra nervously rowed their boat to the bank of the river.

"Hurry, Ezra!"

"I am. Get out a fishing pole."

David quickly scrambled to find a fishing pole under the canvas and wood in the boat.

"Is she changing tack?"

"I can't tell," David responded in a nervous tone.

David and Ezra were making yet another trip to the island. More than once, locals suspiciously eyed the boat loaded with materials. Some pointed and asked questions. Each time, they made the excuse that they were making fishing traps. Obviously the materials were all wrong, but so far, there were no major incidents. They knew, though, that their time and luck would run out if they weren't careful.

"Damn my eyes, she's launching a cutter!"

David watched as the British sloop of war from the in-shore squadron angled up the Connecticut River, obviously looking for Yankee munitions smugglers for the Continental Army. In contrast, the larger ships of the line lazily stood blockade duty. David had heard that the in-shore squadron's sloops were hard working in their search of the many inlets along the coast that harbored privateers and smugglers. Everyone knew that their officers didn't get to attend the social galas in town or even drink ale at a local tavern. They were either chasing suspicious small craft or running dispatches to the admiral.

The sloop's guns looked menacing as it held its position while dropping a cutter over the side. The bright red coats of marines stood out among the checkered shirts of seamen manning the cutter's sail. Ezra and David looked on in horror as the cutter quickly cast off and started to close the half-mile gap between them and the little skiff.

David and Ezra knew that if they tried to run, they would be admitting guilt and quickly gunned down by the marine rifles or swivel gun filled with shot on the bow. Either method ended in a gruesome finish. As the cutter came closer, David could make out what looked like a midshipman in command. At least that was something. The midshipman would probably be in his late teens and not eager to take the initiative to start an incident. On the other hand, he may be extra anxious for promotion to junior lieutenant and quick to show aggression.

"What should we do?" asked David, nearing panic.

"Settle down," calmed Ezra. He was always a counter to David's nerves. "We're just fishing."

"What about all this stuff?" exclaimed an agitated David, pointing at the wood and metal parts in the boat.

"Don't worry, they're looking for guns, powder, and shot—not what we have."

David could see that the cutter's sail was put in irons and flapped aimlessly in the wind to bring the vessel to a stop before their boat. A boatswain's mate threw a line across to Ezra while two marines leveled their guns as a warning. Ezra pulled the line and brought the boat to the cutter while two seamen held out grappling hooks to hold the boat in place.

"Hold steady in the name of a king's officer!" warned the boatswain's mate.

David and Ezra were silent.

"What business have you on this river?" barked the scrawny midshipman. As they expected, he was no older than fifteen. Midshipmen typically entered the Navy by the age of twelve in the hopes of becoming a lieutenant by twenty and a captain by thirty. It was a good career open only to the children of upper-class aristocracy or wealthy middle-class merchants with connections.

"We're fishing, sir," said Ezra with a broad smile.

"What is all that stowage?" asked the midshipman, pointing to the wood.

"We're building a fishing shack to hold our seining in a small camp on a nearby island," confirmed Ezra, coolly referring to fishing nets.

With a nod from the midshipman, a seaman quickly dropped into the boat and rifled through the wood, throwing it casually over the side. It was obvious that the sailor just wanted to start a fight. The midshipman passively looked on while a couple of marines chuckled at the assault.

"Have you seen a Yankee barge making its way upriver?"

It was common knowledge that Yankee merchantmen smuggled stolen munitions or other supplies bought from the French and Spanish up inlets. Barges snuck out to meet them under cover of darkness to unload the cargo and bring it to the local militia.

"No, sir. We would report such a sighting," answered David, trying to act calm.

The midshipman waved the sailor back aboard the cutter.

"If you see any rebel traitors, you tell us and you'll get half a guinea. If you don't, you'll meet a cat-o'-nine-tails," sneered the midshipman, referring to a lashing by an especially painful whip.

Ezra just nodded and said nothing as the seaman pushed off the boat to continue upriver.

David and Ezra tried to quickly maneuver the boat to retrieve the last piece of wood. "At least they didn't throw over the pump," commented Ezra, thinking aloud.

After gathering their floating cargo, the brothers made their way to the island and their water machine. After waiting another hour to ensure that the British were long gone, they uncovered their strange contraption.

David and Ezra had toiled for months and now had an almost finished product, at least theoretically.

They were both in a somber mood as they slowly went about their tasks. Ezra worked to recaulk all joints, especially those that had cracked as they dried. With the anticipated water pressure, there couldn't be a single crack.

David installed the last device. To his frustration, it seemed to stick. He tried several times, but it wasn't consistent in its operation. He was frustrated and finally concluded that he had to return it to Isaac Doolittle, the craftsman who created it.

As David stepped back, he looked at the machine in the morning sun. It was round, almost six feet in height, and about as wide, almost entirely black with pitch and caulk to keep it entirely watertight. It had multiple strange appendages, not unlike sea creatures described by sailors. Just as fish have fins, it contained a large rudder at the backside with similar side protrusions to control motion up and down. Propellers shaped like a corkscrew came out the front and side. The operator had the ability to change the direction of the propeller bars to move the machine forward, back, or sideways. But most prominent was the round, brass head that contained eight small glass windows, six on the outside and two on top to look toward the surface. Also in the brass head protruded two tubes for intake and expiration of air. Inside the tubes were valves that automatically shut off when the machine descended below the surface. Attached was a square wooden magazine, which would later be called a torpedo (after the stinging crampfish Torpedinidae), with an auger and line for attachment to any enemy's hull. When so attached, it would raise a spring to release the torpedo and drop a pin to begin the watch work timer. Also inside was a fixed compass, a ballast of lead (with additional lead ballast on the outside that could be released in an emergency), and a pump to remove that ballast water for ascending to the surface. To tell depth, a rudimentary depth gauge was created with a cork in a water-filled tube. The only thing missing was the defective device that would allow in water for descent and expel water to rise.

"So, that's all that remains," said Ezra, pointing to the opening left from the inoperable pump.

"Yes," confirmed David. "It doesn't work properly. This part, more than the rest, must never fail."

Ezra thought about the implications. "So, if it doesn't work, I can't return to the surface."

David had been so wrapped up in the technical details that he never really contemplated the gruesome implications for Ezra. If any part of the machine didn't work, Ezra would be at the bottom of the ocean under tons of water. His only option was to open the top and try to escape. But that would be impossible with water rushing down on him. In other words, the machine had to work exactly as David theorized or else Ezra would be dead.

"That's correct, Ezra. But I know it will work."

From anyone else, Ezra would have required more. But David communicated differently than most men. When he said it would work, he meant that he knew with absolute certainty that it would work exactly as his mind devised it—even if no man in history had ever attempted it.

It had to work.

Two days and ten miles hence, craftsman Isaac Doolittle wiped his brow before pulling on his huge leather gloves. He needed this protection to grab the pole holding the molten lead in a cup affixed to the rod. He walked three steps to pour the metal into a box containing a sand mold and watched it slowly fill the impression.

With that done, he stopped, needing a break. He walked across the dirt floor to the old wooden door marking the entrance to his shop. The sunlight shone brightly as he stood in front while slipping off his leather apron. Isaac was a craftsman of the first order. He could take a crude drawing and fashion an intricate device. More often than not, he corrected the client's design in the process. Most gadgets were simple. On rare occasions, he got a challenging piece. However, he hadn't gotten any such requests lately—except one.

As he peered at the sporadic passers-by, he saw David Bushnell approach. He liked David and the interesting work he gave him, but he chuckled as he thought about their first meeting. He recalled that he was so difficult to peg. In some ways he looked like a gentleman, but, in other ways, he resembled a farmer. But his drawings were like nothing he'd ever seen before. Unlike those of his other clients, David's drawings were expertly and meticulously done. He obviously had unusual mechanical skills. But the exactness of his designs were matched by his secrecy. Usually Isaac found his clients so enthusiastic about their objects that they couldn't stop talking or gesturing to tell him everything they knew. David was quite the opposite.

"Hello, Mr. Doolittle," said David, now inside his shop.

"Good day, David. I see that you have the device I created. I fear by the look on your face that there might be something wrong."

David felt uncomfortable making a complaint, but he had to ask for a modification. He knew that Isaac was already giving him a break for his services.

"It is a fine work, please don't get me wrong, Mr. Doolittle. However, we had difficulty getting it to work without the mechanism sticking. It has to remove water every time. It cannot fail even once."

Isaac looked skeptical. He had some clients that were difficult to work with and wouldn't accept even the slightest blemish—if for no reason other than pure orneriness. However, David was as amiable as they came, so that couldn't be the reason.

"Normally, I repair tools returned after years of heavy use. Cannot this be the case here?" he asked sincerely, trying to understand.

"No," countered David, equally sincere. "Unfortunately, it must expel water every time without even a single failure—regardless of the stresses it must endure."

Isaac just stared at the device. In the course of their work, David had made him aware of its use in some underwater piece of equipment. However, Isaac had no understanding of the undersea stresses in which it would operate.

David continued. "In looking at the design, the valve mechanism seems to be somewhat different than the original drawing." To illustrate his point, David pulled the drawing and showed the slight variance.

"I see that I may have deviated slightly in the actual manufacture, but no more a variance than is normally done in fashioning metals. Is it that critical?"

David shifted uncomfortably. "Unfortunately, in this vessel, it is very critical, sir. Because of its positioning, it must withstand more pressure than any boat ever made."

Isaac just looked at David. He was sincere, and from the quality of his drawings, Isaac knew that he was extremely precise. He also knew that David seemed to be a man of character and wouldn't return unless the device truly needed to perform as specified.

Isaac looked at the drawing again and then at the device. "I will have to shape the piece from the beginning. I can't alter the existing one—not if you want to contain not even the smallest weak point."

David now looked scared. If that would cost another shilling, David didn't know where he'd obtain the funds. "Sir, as for your fee?"

"We'll conclude that business after I see how long it takes. Is that fair?"

David was uncomfortable. Somehow, having no idea of a fee was worse than knowing the amount of a large one.

"That will be acceptable."

After a few more pleasantries, David left. He frowned with worry. Where would he obtain the funds for another charge from Isaac Doolittle?

CHAPTER 11
PROCESS BEGINS

Tallmadge and Washington reviewed the fruits of their carefully crafted intelligence-gathering process. Woodhull collected the intelligence under the code name Samuel Culper. The first name was created in honor of Tallmadge's deceased brother and the last name from the county of Culpeper, which encompassed Washington's boyhood home. Brewster, with a code number, transported the information when given the signal it was ready at Roe's tavern. Tallmadge received dispatches under the name John Bolton—a common surname respected throughout the colonies.

"So, we now know the precise number of troops garrisoned on Long Island and their exact locations," said Washington with a note of satisfaction.

"Yes, General," affirmed Tallmadge. "Woodhull has done an exceptional job. I fear that he may be doing too good a job. He cannot continue to travel to that extent without raising suspicion."

"I understand," confirmed Washington, "but we need the information."

Both men were well aware that the British were getting thorough in their search of travelers looking for information—often in an effort to elicit any pocket money from the victim. The more honest and diligent in their duties searched books, papers, and even buttons. They knew that any document could be peppered with secret code or invisible lemon juice that could later reappear with the application of heat.

"Thank the Lord that we have our supply of the special reanimater," said Tallmadge, almost in a whisper. Washington was the timely recipient of an invisible ink recently perfected by James Jay. The concept of invisible ink was not new or special. Lemon juice had served this purpose for years. What was new was the reanimater. This ink could only be viewed if a corresponding special reagent was applied that made it visible. Unlike lemon juice, heat had no effect.

"Can you endeavor to get more information on the fleet?" asked Washington. "I need to know their movements, especially the in-shore squadron."

The in-shore squadron, comprised of frigates, sloops, and cutters, was the workhorse of the British fleet. This portion of the fleet was responsible for intercepting information, stopping shipments, and generally strangling the city into submission. More importantly, they were also the ones capable of ultimately breaking Washington's river defenses and landing troops near his forces.

The in-shore squadron operating in the colonies was a problem from the outset when they bombarded the Patriots during the Battle of Bunker Hill. The blockading fleet lay more out to sea, keeping merchant ships out of American ports. However, the Yankee merchantmen often knew their movements and were able to escape to one of thousands of inlets. It was the in-shore squadron that proved their biggest enemy. They patrolled these inlets and, more importantly, punished any innocent colonists they saw as aiding the Patriots in any way.

As they concluded their meeting, Major Tallmadge walked into the night knowing that what they really needed was the ability to drive out the in-shore squadron, not just watch it. For that, they needed a miracle.

CHAPTER 12
DELVING INTO THE DEEP

After yet another clandestine trip to the island, David was the first to climb from the boat and walk to the pile of brush that hid the object of their focus. It was undisturbed. Ezra quickly checked the shack for tampering and found none.

"Where's our new gadget from Mr. Doolittle?" asked Ezra.

David reached for the apparatus hidden in the boat. Then Ezra helped David climb through the opening to install the device. With a final grunt, David managed to install it. From the outside Ezra could hear squeaking while David tested the mechanism. In the next instant, the rudder control, protruding oars (later called bow plains), and propellers were cranked.

David climbed out and they dragged the machine from its resting place into the water with lines and a pulley levered to a tree. As they stood on either side, Ezra peered inside.

"It seems to be water-tight enough. Do you think it will remain so when submerged?"

"Well, one atmosphere is about equal to the pressure of a column of water about fifty feet high, assuming, of course, that the density of seawater is that of freshwater. However, since it's less, the pounds per square inch exerted would be maybe ten. Therefore, we can easily go down more than twenty cables, maybe even some multiple."

"I take it that's a yes, then," countered Ezra.

"Yes," said David. He was accustomed to people giving him a blank stare when he explained some theory or calculation. In many respects, his mind operated in a different place or time—possibly centuries in the future. Ezra and his friend Phineas were perhaps the only two people in the world who could interact with David with any kind of normalcy—Phineas on a limited intellectual level, and Ezra with deep affection.

"I'll get inside while you steady it," directed Ezra.

David held the large rudder while Ezra climbed inside. It was difficult to hold the position given the circular design of the turtle, not like a flat-bottomed boat that offered stability.

David quickly climbed into their rowboat with the line still in hand. "Wait, Ezra, let me get out between you and the river. It will be safer that way."

David pushed off with the boat to get between the water machine and the open water. He didn't want it to get out of control and too far away from shore if there was a problem. Finally, David maneuvered into position while Ezra waited in the machine, his head sticking out the top.

This was more than a test of a new water machine; it was a test of brotherly love. The notion of a machine able to travel underwater like a sea unicorn, or whale, was purely the fancy of a madman. Yet, here Ezra was about to slip below the surface in a homemade machine, created solely from the imagination of his brother. Since no other machine existed of its type, there was no research to be conducted in its design, and no way of verifying engineering principles. This creation came purely from the intuitive understanding of the universe and its inherent dynamics of air, water, gravity, and motion in the mind of David. Only an act of pure love and absolute faith in him could result in Ezra piloting a machine that required his brawn to crank the propeller and other devices.

Ezra took a deep breath.

"Ready?"

"Ready."

"Stay on the surface first to check for leaks and make sure everything works."

Ezra ducked down and sat on the interior stool, with only his eyes showing through the glass spectacles topping the machine. After a pause, he began to crank and the machine lurched forward. David had to move quickly to add slack to the line to stay clear. It zigzagged through the water haphazardly as Ezra cranked with one hand and steered with the other. Finally he seemed to get accustomed to it and moved more gracefully. Before long, it was moving more quickly than David could row. Now about twenty-five yards away, Ezra stood to peer through the top. "David, how fast is that?"

"Maybe three knots?"

"How does it handle?"

"Good. It's a little difficult to get its movements right, but I think I'm learning. It's not easy, though. I don't know how far I'd be able to go before getting too tired. Let's take it out about half a cable and let it descend."

This was the life-or-death moment.

Ezra closed the hatch and was taken aback by how small and enveloped in darkness the machine became. He could hear his breathing resonate off the tiny walls. When they were building the machine, he and David spoke of romantic fantasies about what they might see underwater. When they rowed to and from the island, they joked about finding treasure or discovering new sea creatures. But now things were different. Ezra was hit with the revelation that this was like dropping a coffin to the bottom of nowhere. He thrust open the hatch and gulped air in a panic. David looked on, wide-eyed and concerned. "Are you all right? Is it leaking?"

Ezra was silent for a moment. He knew that if he confessed his fear, David wouldn't let him go. Instead, David would insist on piloting the machine himself. His lack of strength to maneuver the machine or possibly even make it to the surface could really make it become a coffin.

"Yes, I'm fine, David. I was just getting my bearings," he lied.

David didn't understand, but said nothing. Ezra took a breath and closed the hatch again. Like before, the darkness came, but this time Ezra resolved to stay.

"Settle your nerves, Ezra. It's not that far down. Just focus on what David told you," Ezra reasoned out loud as his eyes began to adjust to the shadows. "Here's the ballast handle. Here's the rudder." He squinted and made out the depth device and compass. He stopped to pray. "Lord God in Heaven, please wrap me in angel's wings so I can survive this day."

Ezra opened his eyes again and reached for the ballast handle. Despite his shaking hand, he found himself mechanically moving as they had practiced on land. At first nothing happened, so he moved it further. Suddenly water started rushing in much faster than expected and the machine descended like a rock.

"Oh, God. It's going too fast!" exclaimed Ezra. Ezra closed the valve, but it was already too late.

His first impulse was to open the hatch and swim for it. He even put both hands on the hatch in a panic. It was almost surreal as he heard the sounds of his own terrified utterances, sounding like a wounded animal caught in a trap. But he was jolted as the machine hit the bottom and his head banged the hull only inches away. The shock seemed to bring him back in control as the round machine rolled forward. Ezra braced himself, waiting for it to turn upside down, but it rolled back into place.

Ezra tried to calm his nerves by repeating the instructions given by David. "Pump the water out and watch the depth gauge." Ezra felt in the cold ocean water for the ballast pump.

It was hard to move and creaked with the strain. Ezra pumped slowly and then more rapidly, but the water still covered his feet.

"Please, please work." He continued to pump but paused to look at the tiny cork in the tube that measured depth. In his panic, he hadn't taken note of the position when the machine settled on the bottom and now couldn't tell if it had changed. He stared longer, but it didn't move.

"Please, Lord," he repeated, becoming panicky again. At some point, he'd have to open the hatch and try to escape before air ran out, but there were still several more minutes left. He pumped again and stared at the device.

Back on the surface, David too was in a panic. Ezra was only to descend about two fathoms. He was at least four, and virtually out of sight.

Initially David screamed, "Ezra! Ezra!" as if Ezra could hear him.

David began to pull on the line with all his might. It was only a few seconds, but as his mind raced it felt like a hundred lifetimes.

David continued to yell, "Ezra! Ezra!" There was nothing.

David began to cry. He pulled on the line again but it wouldn't move. He changed his position and laid flat on his chest, pulling on the line. Again nothing. He started taking off his coat to swim to the machine, but stopped. Even if he could reach that depth, he couldn't raise the heavy machine. He went back to his position and pulled on the line again. Finally, the line started to have slack and he could barely make out a dark, black form rising in the depths. It was coming up. Hopefully Ezra was alive.

Suddenly the machine popped through the surface like a cork. The hatch flung open and Ezra emerged, white as a ghost and out of breath.

"Are you all right?" asked David excitedly.

Hyperventilating, Ezra quickly looked around as if making sure he was really on the surface. "I'm fine," he said finally. "I let in too much water and it descended farther than I wanted. I hit the bottom, hard."

"Did it stick to the bottom?"

"No, thank God. When I pumped out the water, I could feel that I was rising."

"That might have been me. I pulled on the line."

They looked at each other in confusion. Did the ballast device work, or was it David? The whole experience was nothing like David had fantasized about. No new discoveries under the sea. No treasures or shipwrecks; only terror.

They silently towed the machine back to the island and hid the machine as if not wanting to relive the experience. Finally they sat. The lack of activity made speaking of the event a requirement.

"What's next?" asked David.

Ezra slowly shook his head at the thought of doing it again. "I don't know."

CHAPTER 13
EXTORTION BY ANOTHER NAME

"It's hard to imagine professional officers acting in such a way. It's as if they have no conscience at all," growled Washington with disgust.

"Yes, General," responded Tallmadge, shaking his head.

"Pray, continue."

"According to Woodhull [alias Culper Senior], General Burgoyne wrote letters to the British secretary of state complaining about the inactivity of his counterpart in the blockading squadron, Admiral Graves."

"I'm not surprised. Burgoyne's a cur that would blame the Almighty if it shielded him from retribution," affirmed Washington.

"Yes, General," continued Tallmadge. "Woodhull stated that Burgoyne charged Graves with not supplying needed food and ammunition, not defending ports, and not dispatching urgent communications."

"That is certainly true," interrupted Washington. "No man in the fleet even sees the admiral. He's too busy enjoying Manhattan's social life."

"The letters must have found their mark, because shortly thereafter Woodhull reports that Graves was ordered to take action. But, to everyone's surprise, Graves commanded a detachment of ships to bombard a small coastal town rather than trying to stop the flow of arms by privateers, like the inshore squadron."

"Not a scrap of honor among them," grunted Washington.

"It gets worse, General. On arrival, the British sent word to the town that they must deliver an emissary to hear their demands within one hour, or they would level the city. We understand that Governor Bradford was there to receive the request and was confused as to why the British fleet would be making demands of a civilian town, rather than the enemy. He replied to the messenger that it would be more appropriate for a British senior officer to come ashore, where they would be pleased to show him some hospitality and discuss the apparent confusion. On hearing the message, the ship's captain obviously disagreed and began the broadsides. The town's leaders gathered in Bradford's office along with the colonel of the militia. Governor Bradford sent a lieutenant from the militia in a long boat to meet with the British. I understand that the British demanded two hundred sheep and thirty cattle to stop the bombardment."

"That's outrageous," exclaimed Washington. "So, when charged with not delivering supplies from Europe, General Burgoyne bombed a local town to get it. It's truly a crime."

"Apparently, but the Patriot lieutenant gave him a run for his money and offered ten sheep, stating that with the economy so poor, that was all they could muster," said Tallmadge, now laughing.

Washington joined him. "The Captain obviously hadn't bargained on Americans having the gall to negotiate a bribe."

"Yes, General," continued Tallmadge. "In the end, the British agreed to leave for forty sheep. In fact, I understand that the townspeople already wrote a poem to commemorate the event."

"Read it," encouraged a wide-eyed Washington.

Tallmadge cleared his throat and read aloud from a paper,

With all their firing and their skill
They did not any person kill,
Neither was any person hurt
Except the Reverend parson Burt,
And he was not killed by a ball,
As judged by jurors one and all.
But being in a sickly state,
He frightened fell, which proved his fate.

Laughing aside, the British fleet moved from simply blockading New York to extorting payment from local towns at gunpoint. The situation for civilians was getting worse.

Fifty miles distant, things likewise worsened for the intelligence report's author. A detachment of Queen's Rangers surrounded Abraham Woodhull's family home. When it was clear that all escape routes were covered, the man in charge, Colonel Simcoe, approached the house.

"Abraham Woodhull," he shouted from twenty-five yards in front of the house, "we order you to come out in the name of the king."

There was no answer. Richard Woodhull, Abraham's elderly father, peered out the window.

"What should we do?" asked his grandson earnestly.

"All we can do is let them in."

The elder Woodhull gently opened the door and descended onto the porch.

"Are you Abraham Woodhull?" asked an incredulous Colonel Simcoe a few feet away.

"No, I'm Richard Woodhull. My son Abraham is not here. He's in New York visiting his sister." It was true. Abraham was not in the area.

"You're lying," chimed the indignant colonel. "He's hiding

with his cowardly brothers, no doubt."

"My other two sons are dead. He has no brothers," retorted the old man in almost a guttural tone.

Furious, Simcoe ordered his men to tear apart the house looking for Abraham. He then took the family one by one into a room for interrogation. The old man took the brunt of the questions—most delivered with a backhand across the face. Each family member proclaimed Abraham's innocence and the colonel finally gave up. He had the old man dragged out to the front yard and ordered Woodhull's family to watch the corporal punishment.

"This is what we do to anyone related to a Yankee traitor," Simcoe announced, directing the men to beat the old man, who finally fell silently to the ground.

Days later, Abraham slowly approached the house. He was still reeling from having some British officers suddenly quartered at the home where he stayed to conduct his business, making his reports to Washington that much more precarious. Every report was done immediately on the other side of a wall from the sleeping enemy. On top of that, he had been recently robbed by a highwayman. Colonials were reverting to thievery themselves to survive. As he approached, he could see his father hobbling around with the aid of a family member.

"What's happened?"

"It's nothing. We were paid a visit by the British. I'm just grateful that you weren't here. You may have been granted Georgia parole," replied his father.

Abraham knew instantly what he meant. "Georgia parole" was a phrase referring to execution of a prisoner by the military without granting quarter. It was such a common practice by colonial militia in the southern colonies that it gained the name, known to all. His father went on to explain the beating and message meant for his son.

It was unclear how the British came to suspect Woodhull. It

could have been his frequent trips to Manhattan, Brewster's boat always leaving on urgent business following his return, or one too many evenings spent in Roe's tavern. It could also be that he was just any number of colonists caught up in an ongoing campaign of intimidation designed to deter any help for the Patriots.

But the conclusion was clear: the walls were closing in on him.

CHAPTER 14
WORKING CAPITAL

David walked into the Yale Library. Phineas was studying but looked up as David approached, anxiously awaiting the results of his underwater machine experiment. He withdrew with David to a corner for privacy.

"So, how was it?"

David struggled to find the right words. "It seemed to operate correctly, but the ballast pump didn't regulate the intake and expulsion of ballast properly. The water came in too fast."

"Oh?" asked Phineas, wondering the fate of Ezra.

"But Ezra's fine. It was scary for a while," answered David.

"I'm sure," said Phineas, picturing the situation, "especially for Ezra. But he's fine?"

"Yes, we were both shaken, but it worked."

"When can I see it?"

"It's still too dangerous, and besides, I need to alter the design to make it operate more slowly."

Phineas was silent. He knew David had meager funds, unlike himself.

"Can I spot you a few shillings?"

"Oh, no," responded David, shaking his head emphatically. "I'd never be able to pay you back."

"What about the local colonial authorities? You're far enough along to at least approach them."

"I've thought about that, but who'd believe me? An underwater ship? Worse yet, what if they did believe me and turned out to be secret Loyalists?"

Phineas looked down. "Yes, yes, I suppose so. What about if you choose a lower-level official? You could claim it was a joke if he tried to turn you in."

David thought for a second. "I'm not sure I want to risk my neck on that."

"Well, I don't know, David. At some point you have to take a chance. Either now and obtain funds to finish the machine, or risk it being found later by the in-shore squadron. Besides, you have to approach the authorities at some point to bring it into action."

Now David was silent. The logic was there, as painful as it was. But still, it was risky. Finally Phineas concluded, "Well, you think about it."

Phineas went back to study while David went to his room at the boardinghouse. The more he thought about it, the more he realized that if he inquired now, at least he'd protect Ezra from the British by claiming to have developed it alone. If he waited and they got caught together in the river, Ezra would hang with him, and they'd never help the war effort. He had to do something.

The next day, David sat quietly in the outer office of a local official representing the Connecticut Safety Council with his drawing neatly under his arm. Long minutes soon turned into an hour. With no apparent activity in the office, it seemed that the official obviously thought little of a Yale student with a proposal. David looked at the paintings adorning the wall, once again analyzing their details. There were only two and the third was missing—probably an official of the Crown now out of favor because of the revolution, thought David.

As David sat, he got both angry and frustrated. But he was desperate for money, so much so as to accept the insult and wait a while longer. Finally an assistant walked through the door at the end of the small hall. He was startled when he saw David still sitting there. Despite being the one who had instructed David to wait, he attempted a crooked smile and went back through the door whence he came. Obviously they'd hoped David would have given up and left.

Within minutes the assistant appeared again and beckoned David into an office. Apparently, the assistant told his boss that David wasn't leaving and he could put it off no longer.

The official continued to look down at his papers. He was about David's age but by the look of him, probably the son of a prominent merchant. The assistant announced, "Mr. David Bushnell," but with no reaction. Finally the official, seemingly inconvenienced, waved in the direction of the chair. David sat, but decided not to speak until the official at least looked up from his desk. It was a way of maintaining at least some dignity.

Finally the young aristocrat stood up and growled loudly, "It's so blasted hot in here. Where's that useless assistant of mine? I'll do it myself." He flung open the window.

David had thought it felt quite pleasant. Obviously this man needed to exert what little power he had.

He turned to David. "Well, sir. What exactly are you seeking from the colonial government?"

David quickly tried to recall what he'd practiced in his mind, but began to blurt it out as best he could, "I...I, well actually my brother and I have created this water machine. Well, we are not actually finished, but almost there. It's to help drive the British fleet from Boston, by destroying a ship."

The official just looked at him. Obviously they weren't connecting.

David stood and unrolled his drawing, trying not to spill the ink well in the center of the desk. "You see, sir, the machine can travel underwater to deliver a keg of gunpowder to a ship." He pointed to the torpedo in the drawing. "You see, sir, it gets attached to the hull."

The official looked as if he was about to summon a guard. Then David noticed the official's shifty smile that could, at any moment, erupt into laughter.

David continued, "Sir, I've demonstrated the exploding device at Yale. The professors can vouch for it."

Finally the official said, "You want money, is that it?"

David stammered, "Yes, sir, just enough to finish the machine…and maybe for some food." As quickly as he said it, he regretted it. Now he sounded like some sort of starving vagabond and a fool.

They both stood silent. Finally the man said, "Do you have some sort of letter describing your…. machine?"

"Yes, sir," said David, retrieving a letter from his pocket.

"We'll let you know, Mr…." He had to look at the bottom of the letter. "Mr. Bushnell."

David quietly rolled up his drawing in silence as the man continued to smirk. David closed the door as he left and actually made it three steps before the man's hysterical laughter echoed through the room. The assistant just looked at David with a scornful grin.

David almost ran from the building, humiliated. He stopped and sat on the steps with a mixture of anger and disgust, feeling violated. His fantasies, where the official was supposed to gather congressmen and generals alike to marvel at his work, were crushed. Maybe he should have never left the farm. Now, he had to worry about his letter getting passed around as a joke with the potential of reaching the British.

CHAPTER 15
AMERICA'S FIRST SUPER SPY

After being nearly captured and with his nerves in a knot, Woodhull knew that another spy had to be recruited to assume part of the load. It was obvious that his alias, Culper Senior, could no longer visit Manhattan with regularity. He had to find a new agent within Manhattan's affluent circles to eavesdrop on the conversations of British senior officers and government officials in social settings. At the same time, the spy recruit had to be strategically located to observe ship comings and goings in addition to troop deployments. Most of all, the new spy had to come and go from New York to deliver information to a courier without suspicion. Nobody fit the bill better than Robert Townsend.

Townsend's mild manner and propensity to be lost in books made him seem like the unlikeliest of candidates. However, his placement within a prominent Long Island family was the first step toward meeting Washington's requirements. His conversion to spy was now possible because of a series of events that forced his hand.

Robert Townsend was the fourth son of a well-to-do father who presided over a family business that conducted trade between America and Europe. The eldest brother, Solomon, was assumed to eventually take over the role as patriarch after having proven himself commanding the family's merchant ships. The second and third sons likewise rose to prominence managing various parts of the family's affairs. In contrast, Robert quietly maintained ledgers and inspected shipments in the background. In an attempt to transform his reclusive son, the elder Townsend secured an apprenticeship at a merchant house in the lively "Holy Ground" district of Manhattan. The name stood in contrast to the real nature of the area known for brothels and all manner of activates associated with an active New York waterfront. Despite the area, Robert maintained his Puritan-like habits while distinguishing himself with his hard work and industry.

After a time, Robert became a merchant himself, running a shop and travelling between Long Island and New York to acquire and deliver merchandise. However, it was on these visits that Robert Townsend became a revolutionary. His father, Samuel Townsend Sr., had been known as an outspoken opponent of the Crown for its abuse of the American Colonies. This prominence eventually brought about his beating by the very same Colonel Simcoe who had beaten the elder Abraham Woodhull, alias Culper Senior's father. Furthermore, Simcoe took over the Townsend family estate to quarter his troops. Robert witnessed firsthand the officers and men that inhabited the house, with his father and sisters relegated to back rooms and the subject of much derision.

"So, your father was beaten by the good Colonel Simcoe of the Queens Rangers just like my own?" said Woodhull.

"Yes," responded Townsend with an icy stare.

"What say ye then? A serving of revenge in addition to helping our good General Washington?"

"Yes," responded the reserved Townsend. "Revenge it shall be."

The walls may have been closing in on Woodhull, but his work would continue, and he'd have some measure of revenge on the man who had made it so personal.

CHAPTER 16
THE HEADMASTER

As David made his way to class, the headmaster approached. "Mr. Bushnell."

A startled David answered, "Yes, sir."

"I just wanted to check on our favorite pupil." This was a surprise given that David was not in the habit of ever talking to the headmaster.

"I'm fine, sir."

"Good. Would you have a moment to come with me?"

"Of course."

David nervously followed the headmaster to a relatively modest but comfortable office. Red oak furniture filled the small area, with bookshelves surrounding the room from ceiling to floor. Each shelf displayed an assortment of books and an eclectic collection of specimens that included bones and various decorative items from different cultures. But David was drawn to the books, many of which he recognized from his studies. He found himself staring at a few volumes on the shelves.

"I can see that you are well acquainted with the classic philosophies," said the headmaster as an icebreaker.

"Yes, thank you, sir, I am," answered David.

David realized the uncomfortable silence called for him to speak again. "Certainly some of the books have a bearing on today."

"Oh, how so?" asked the headmaster, seeing an apparent opening.

Now David was in a fix. When he made the statement, he hadn't quite considered the ramifications. He quickly searched the books for a title and a relevant comment.

"Jean Jacques Rousseau and his discussion of personal liberty being restricted by government has a basis in the creation of the Patriot movement doctrine today." There, he had addressed a political topic without taking a stand.

"And, the conflict surrounding an abuse of power by the king," added the headmaster. With that said, he seemed to be leaning toward independence, but still left doubt. He continued, "David, I wanted to see how your experiments with gunpowder and a practical application are progressing."

David was shocked by the awareness of his actions. He didn't know the affiliation of the headmaster. If the headmaster were a Tory and David answered that they were going well, the master would logically piece together the plot to attack the British fleet. On the other hand, if he were a Patriot, a man in his position may be able to help with needed funds. David took a chance by leaning, just slightly, in the direction of the Patriots.

"My experiments are going fairly well."

The headmaster was determined to learn more.

"I know you were able to detonate gunpowder under water with devastating effect. Have you perfected some sort of machine to transport gunpowder to a target?"

That was a very direct question. Had he somehow learned about David's work on the island? Or, more likely, gotten wind of the letter to the Connecticut Council of Safety? Either way, David had to lie outright to avoid danger and possibly forego help, or tell the truth and let the chips fall where they may.

Again, David tried to be honest, but slightly evasive. "My machine is close, sir."

The headmaster seemed to make a noncommittal sign of appreciation. David had confirmed the nature of his work and that he was close to success. If the master were a fervent Patriot, he was fine; or he would go to the gallows if he was a Tory. Showing no emotion, the headmaster said, "I want you to share your ideas with my friend, Dr. Gale."

David knew the doctor, as did almost everyone, or at least those in the neighboring colonies. He was a well-known researcher and physician.

"For any particular reason, sir?"

"I just want him to see you, and to *see it*."

David didn't know what to say. What did this mean?

"Mr. Bushnell, I fear that I've made you hopelessly late for class. Your teacher would never forgive me if I detained you any longer. I'll have my associate give you directions to his house." He waved his arm toward the door in a very direct, but polite, order to leave.

David left the room with mixed feelings, some panic, and some confusion. After class, he'd have to sort it out.

It seemed that the day of classes would never end—now more than most days. When David had started at Yale, his classes seemed interesting. Now, with all his spare time, money, and effort consumed by his water machine, classes were just a nuisance. If he weren't a senior and that much closer to a diploma, he'd probably have quit. His spare time was spent going over the mechanical operation of the device in any situation, making plans, and trying to remember things to tell Ezra. If a current were to capsize the machine under water, what should he do to right it? What if it got caught in some sort of underwater riptide? How should he try to gain control? The possibilities for failure seemed endless. This was the ocean. As David walked next to the tiny Yale campus, he tried to clear his mind.

"Well, Master Bushnell," chided Phineas, coming up from behind.

"Phineas," stammered David in surprise.

"Where have you been anyway? Playing in puddles again, I fear."

"The headmaster's chambers. He knows about the water machine," croaked David, drawing the attention of passersby.

"How does he know?" whispered a doubtful Phineas

"I don't know. Maybe someone at the library saw the drawings. Maybe somebody saw us on the river," David conjectured. "Or, maybe somebody knows we're building it and wants the headmaster to find out if it's a real threat."

"Settle down, David. Everyone knows that Dr. Gale is friends with Benjamin Franklin and the Continental Congress. If the headmaster was a Tory, he wouldn't send you to the doctor."

"I suppose so. So you think I should go?"

"If you think the machine's ready."

"We have to practice some more, but it's generally ready. The only thing not tested is the new pump and the gunpowder magazine."

"How does that work?"

"I've installed a corkscrew that can be operated from underwater and detach the magazine from the machine and onto the ship."

"It sounds like you can go to Dr. Gale now."

"I'm still nervous. There's a lot of people that play both sides and aren't what they seem. I need you to find out anything you can about Dr. Gale. You have connections that I don't."

"So, I'm to be a spy?"

"Actually, yes." Even David's analytical mind couldn't escape that conclusion.

"I'll do it!" Now Phineas turned to his more playful nature. "David, you really need a name for that thing."

"Why?" Being so analytical and fixated on the operational theory behind his invention, the idea of a name was completely foreign. "You mean like a warship?"

"Yes, exactly."

David thought for a minute. "Well, we have said that it looks like a turtle, with its black outer hull and circular form."

"Actually, David, I was thinking something more manly like *Avenger* or *The Devil's Teeth*," laughed Phineas, "but *Turtle* will be just fine."

CHAPTER 17
DR. GALE

The leaves were blowing around his feet as he walked on the dirt path leading to the large house. David could see a few lamps lit in the stately house. It was bordering on poor manners to make a social call at such an hour, but David thought to escape into the night at the first sign of trouble. He climbed the porch steps and reached the door, knocking three times. At first there was no sound. He almost turned around and walked away, taking it as a bad omen. Then he could make out the faint sounds of footsteps in the back of the house. Strangely, the light emanating from the windows was almost gone as the resident extinguished the gaslights as he went. Adding to the strangeness, David realized that the footsteps weren't far at all. The walker, whoever it was, had removed his shoes to make less noise. Only the sound of the creaking floor gave his position away, directly opposite David on the other side of the door. But still there was silence as if the person was waiting for something.

David had a feeling of dread and quickly decided to leave. Whatever was happening, he didn't want to be the subject of their next actions. Just as quickly as he turned, the door bolt loudly slammed and the door creaked open, just a crack.

"What do you want?"

"I'm here to see Dr. Gale."

"Are you ill?"

"No, sir, I'm here on business."

"Government business?"

"No, private business."

"Is it just you?"

David quickly wondered what he should do. Should he lie and say somebody was with him for protection? As he thought, his hesitation went on too long.

Finally, David admitted, "I'm alone, sir."

Now the silence from the other side was deafening and equally uncomfortable as the other person obviously debated what action to take next.

David added, "If another time would be more convenient?"

"No, no," came the reply, "now is convenient."

The door finally opened halfway. David could barely make out the form of the man in the shadows. He wasn't large and David might be able to handle him if he had to escape.

"Come in, come in. I'll give us some light."

David cautiously entered the darkness of the room, partially shielding his head in case the man planned a blow. He could make out the figure walking along the back wall to an adjoining room to light a gas lamp. With the flick of his wrist, there was light and David could see him. He was almost elderly and well dressed. He seemed to be a man of means.

"I'm sorry, but these days you never can be too careful. I'm Doctor Gale. What can I do for you?"

"I'm David Bushnell from Yale College. I've come to, um… about an experiment?" This was the most difficult part. David didn't know exactly what the headmaster intended.

The doctor instantly perked up, his graying hair and slightly rotund body becoming more youthful in an instant. "Are you conducting some kind of experiments into the natural philosophies?" Dr. Gale was well known in the colonies as a premier researcher and a recipient of the Royal Society's Gold Medal.

"Yes, sir. It involves traveling under water."

David wondered if he was going to be laughed out of the room.

"I've heard a fantastic notion from my friend at Yale. I also heard a letter was making its way to the Continental Congress. So, it's actually true?"

"Yes, sir," said David with an urge to flee.

Sensing his discomfort, Dr. Gale consoled, "You're safe here, young man."

David was still unsure. "How do I know that you won't turn me over to the British?" he asked directly.

"I suppose you don't. All I can say is that because of my research into the natural philosophies, I've become friends with others of similar interests like Benjamin Franklin and, of course, your headmaster. And as you know, our esteemed Mr. Franklin is a well-known member of the Continental Congress."

"Yes, I, of course, know much of Mr. Franklin." Benjamin Franklin was perhaps the best-known American in the world. His work with electricity and his publication of several newspapers and *Poor Richard's Almanack* was common knowledge. "I was also advised that you were a friend of his. That's partly why I'm here."

"Is it now?" said the doctor, surprised. If David knew of their relationship, then why was he so jumpy?

Almost reading his thoughts, David said, "I'm sorry for my behavior. The lamps being out unnerved me. And, you never can be too careful. Many people who seem to be Patriots are actually Tories in disguise. Especially people of some wealth as yourself."

"I understand," said the doctor, now seated again. "So, how can I be of service?"

"I believe that my headmaster sent me because he knew that the water machine is almost ready."

"Bless my eyes, is it?" Now the researcher in Dr. Gale burst out with a barrage of excited questions. "How do you rise and descend?"

"I've created a pump that lets in water to descend and removes it when we wish to rise toward the surface."

"Amazing. But when you remove the water, there's still enough air to make the thing rise?"

"Yes. When you let in the water, the air remains and becomes compressed into a smaller space. I think it becomes heavier, but I'm not entirely sure."

"And, how do you propel yourself under the surface? There is no sail, of course."

"I've designed turning pieces of metal that push the water out of the way, forward and backward."

"Really? How do you know where you're going?"

"I made a device to measure how deep it is. It also has a compass to show direction, and windows to see."

"How do you get more air?"

"Through another tube at the top."

Finally the doctor was silent, seemingly looking for more obstacles. Then his eyes lit up.

"My God. You have done it!" exclaimed the doctor, now on his feet. "When can I see it?"

"In a few days if you wish. My brother and I will demonstrate it."

"Excellent."

"If you see it, you can tell Mr. Franklin. Since he is involved in the Patriot movement at the highest levels, he can tell Mr. Washington. Our funding is low and we need help," said David, lost in the moment.

"Yes, of course. Then you have a bomb of sorts that goes with the machine?"

"Yes, sir."

Now the doctor was silent. "Pity. For a moment I almost forgot we were at war. I was only thinking of the possibilities of exploring the undersea world."

David just chuckled. He thought the doctor was making a joke, but the doctor didn't seem to take offense.

"Of course, you'll stay here tonight. You look thin and pale. I'll ring for some food." The doctor was automatically turned to his medical inclinations as they walked up the stairs together.

It appeared that David had made a friend. More importantly, he'd finally gotten the reaction he had dreamed of.

CHAPTER 18
THE SUPER SPY BECOMES A MOLE

Mild-mannered Robert Townsend, now code named Culper Junior, took over much of the intelligence gathering for Culper Senior. However, it was primarily limited to what he could gather in his shop and the nearby waterfront. What came next was a point of brilliance.

Near Townsend's business was a coffeehouse owned by James Riverton. More importantly in the back of the coffeehouse was Riverton's print shop. Like many printers, Riverton published a newspaper with articles written by himself and those collected from various contributors, ranging from political editorials to poems. In fact, one regular submitter of poems was Major John Andre, popularly known throughout town as a charismatic and fun-loving British officer. Unknown in town was his role as spymaster for the British and the direct counterpart of Washington's spymaster, Major Tallmadge. Just as important, the newspaper was firmly Tory, publishing all articles and opinion columns in favor of the British. Anyone working for the paper was well placed to gather information above suspicion.

Being a keen writer himself, Townsend began to submit literary pieces often critical of the Patriots. These pieces became popular with the newspaper, which offered him a position as reporter. His alter ego, Culper Junior, now had the perfect opportunity to ask questions of British officers and government officials alike rather than waiting to eavesdrop on conversations himself. This cover likewise allowed him to travel anywhere around New York, observing and taking notes as he pleased. The information for Washington was now detailed and from the source—some coming from the British spymaster Major John Andre himself.

It was a stroke of pure luck that the British spymaster frequented the paper at the same time as Townsend. Major Andre had come to the notice of his superior because of his savvy and worldly charisma. Andre's parents hailed from Paris and Geneva respectively, giving Andre the ability to speak multiple languages and mix socially in the highest circles. Just as important, he was endowed with dashing good looks that attracted the affection of more than one colonial lady, including Peggy Shippen, the soon-to-be-wife of Benedict Arnold. Among other talents, Andre fancied himself a poet and found a ready publicist in the paper.

Townsend was quick to make the acquaintance of the British spymaster to gain any intelligence he could. This association also allowed him to observe who else associated with the spymaster. In this way, he came to know who was a Patriot and who a closet Loyalist feeding information to the British. Probably most of all, he was introduced to who would become America's first female spy and a kingpin of Washington's ring. Her beauty was only matched by her guile. But, events would soon transpire to require the combined skills of both to the test.

CHAPTER 19
THE SEA TRIAL

David, Ezra, and the doctor watched as an armed British patrol walked along the road. In the front were six men heavily bearded and dressed in animal skins. Their features looked sun baked and greasy. Their furs were covered in mud and grime. Despite their unkempt appearance, they were probably even more feared than redcoats. They were Canadians.

David's family had seen some action against Canadians in the French and Indian War. Even in that conflict, it was determined that whichever army mastered the wilderness mastered the war. The Patriots drew upon Native Americans, who knew their environments and how to use topography to their advantage in battle. Young braves were taught from childhood to track game and deal with the hazards, fatigue, and hardships while constantly improving their hunting skills. These skills proved invaluable in warfare and, most of all, gathering intelligence on enemy positions as a scout. Indian scouts, for the most part, were lightly armed, highly mobile, and extremely resourceful in terms of supplying themselves while on campaign. They had knowledge of terrain that the Army couldn't hope to gain within a short span of time. Native scouts and their tactical knowledge became legendary. Even David and Ezra learned as children the Indian tactics and stealth in make-believe war games with their cousins.

Everyone knew that the British Army was no stranger to the need for good scouts. Since the Americans had exclusive access to native Indians to act as scouts, the British sent to Canada for frontiersmen with wilderness stealth of their own. The Canadian trappers were almost equally quick to master terrain, hunt in silence, and find the enemy. Probably more than anything else, they were known for their ruthlessness in killing. More than one American had his throat slit while quietly standing guard duty. Often the distinction between the military and civilians was ignored in the confusion. For that reason, the mere sight of the Canadian scouts meant that pain and suffering would soon follow.

As they passed, Ezra growled under his breath, "Damned, godless animals."

"Be quiet, Ezra," whispered David.

As they watched, the patrol continued up the road until it disappeared in the neighboring bush. The sight of the group made everyone ill at ease. Would they be watched as they made for their island and the water machine? A Canadian could probably hide right next to their contraption without their ever knowing it, until it was too late. Before they could run, the scout's knife could do its worst.

"We best be off," said Ezra, getting the group to move.

"Are you sure?" asked the doctor.

"Yes, we're probably safer now that we know they're about than if we hadn't seen them at all. If we were their target, we'd already be dead." It was little consolation, but accepted anyway.

It was approaching dusk in a few hours when the three climbed into the boat and began their trek to Poverty Island. The water was relatively smooth, with the boat rocking slowly on the crest of each wave. It was a good day to test the *Turtle*. The group was silent, partly from the sight of a patrol and partly because they were going to do a full test, with Ezra deep under water. The silence was only broken by seagulls looking for a free meal.

When they finally reached the island, they found the *Turtle* undisturbed. The doctor instantly started to examine each detail.

"This is how it moves up and down?" he asked, pointing at the pump on the inside. "Yes, and this," said David, pointing at the propeller screw at the top.

"How long have you had it under water?"

"Only thirty minutes."

"That seems very long. Will you do that tonight?"

"I figured that we would have Ezra descend with the machine under water and steer a course for about that long. We'll be in the boat above with a rope in case he has any difficulty surfacing."

"How will you know if he's in trouble?"

"I assumed we'd watch from the surface, aided with this glass bottom mug to see beneath."

"It seems simple enough."

Finally, a sloop appeared in the darkness under the command of Caleb Brewster, the primary courier of Washington's spy ring. With the sloop they could test the *Turtle* in different waters, more like those near the British fleet.

"Ready, gents?" said Brewster. Dr. Gale and the others knew nothing of Brewster's role for the spy ring. They only knew he had been arranged as transport by a friend.

"It looks awfully cramped in there," said Dr. Gale, looking over the side into the *Turtle*. It was obvious that any man with enough nerve to go beneath the surface in this untried machine was stupid, crazy, or both. He shuddered at the thought of being trapped in there.

"It's big enough," said Ezra, dropping in. The sloop pulled deep into the river, as agreed, while David went over the plan.

"Ezra, go below the surface for fifteen minutes trailing the sloop to demonstrate its ability to navigate and attack a warship undetected." Then David turned to the doctor. "Just see if you can spot him."

When they were far enough, David gave the signal to Brewster, who said to slow and let the *Turtle* go.

Ezra took two deep breaths. It was obvious that he was very nervous. David likewise was scared.

"Are you sure you want to go through with this, Ezra?" whispered David.

"Yes, we worked too long, too hard and took too many chances to get this far. It's now or never."

With that, Ezra abruptly closed the hatch.

David and Dr. Gale waited until they could see him through the small glass eyes on the *Turtle*.

Before they could react and process exactly what they were doing, the *Turtle* descended below the water.

"Is it all right?" asked Dr. Gale.

"I think so."

The sloop hoisted only a jib to begin a slow move up the river.

Thirty minutes passed with no sign of Ezra.

"Is he still all right?"

"I think so," said David, mechanically repeating himself again.

"How long has it been now, David?"

"More than forty minutes, I think."

"He better come up soon." Now David's excitement turned to near panic. "Captain Brewster, please stop the sloop."

The men hauled down the jib and the sloop slowed to a stop.

Suddenly, the *Turtle* surfaced just feet away. The hatch opened and Ezra emerged. "Did you see me?"

"I'll be damned. You were right behind us all that time?" laughed Brewster.

"Yes," returned Ezra, out of breath. "It was hard to see, though. A couple times I almost ran into the hull. We'll have to work on that."

The sailors were now standing near Brewster, dumbfounded, and commenting under their breath about the strange machine.

"Let's get back to shore and talk," said David, now nervous. He wasn't used to having their covert activities observed by people he didn't know.

Now the doctor was almost jumping with excitement. Ezra was too tired from cranking the screw so they tied a line and towed the *Turtle* to back where they had started. Ezra slumped inside, enjoying the tow. Reaching the island, they dragged their new invention onto the beach.

"Amazing. Just amazing! What was it like down there?" asked the doctor.

Ezra sat on a nearby log while the two huddled around him.

"It's always difficult to adjust initially. It's a small space, and the foxwood produces just enough of a glow to see the devices." Foxwood, found in the forest, contained a phosphorous fungus producing a luminous effect at night.

Ezra continued, "I was especially nervous because I was going into the open sea for the first time. When the sloop pulled me out into the river, I calmed down and reached for the pump to go down. But just as we designed it, the water stopped when I let the cork reach a depth one-third of the way down on the device. Then I moved the propeller to keep pace with the lamps that lit the sloop's deck. I kept track of the time in each direction by counting. Then after it seemed to be moving well and keeping pace, I let in more water to go further down. After going a little ways, I thought I was pretty far down. About that time the sloop stopped."

Now the doctor was talking in frenzy. "We have to get news of this to Doctor Franklin and the Continental Congress. This is a great achievement for the colonies."

Ezra turned to David. "I believe it's time to bring in Mr. Franklin."

"Could you discreetly tell Mr. Franklin enough of this machine to make these things happen, without arousing the whole Congress?" asked David.

"Absolutely, young man. I'll go straight away and have a courier deliver a message to our esteemed inventor. He'll know what to do."

Without realizing the significance of their first undersea journey, the Bushnell brothers had perfected the fundamentals of future submarines. They developed a crude version of a ballast tank, a device for measuring their depth under water, and the means to navigate the vessel—and they perfected the propeller. Man's knowledge of the sea would be expanded a millionfold with their discovery. Yet, the world couldn't know of their achievement.

Dear Mr. Franklin,

Your Congress doubtless have Intimations of the Invention of a new Machine for the Destruction of Ships of War. I now sit down to Give you an Acct of that Machine and what Experiments have been Already made with it what I relate you may Intirely rely upon to be fact. I will not at this Time attempt to Give You a Minute Description of the Form, as the Post is now Waiting. Thus Much, it doth not Exceed 7 feet in Length, and the Depth not more then 5½ feet, the Person who Navigates it, sits on a Bench in the Center of the Machine. The Person who Invented it, is a Student of Yale Colledge, and is Graduated this Year. Lives within five Mile of me. I was the second Person who ever was permitted to see it, there being no other Workman but himself and Brother, Excepting what Iron Work is wanted, which was done by His direction. His Plan is to place the Cask Containing the Powder on the Outside of the Machine, and it is so Contrived, as when it strikes the Ship, which he proposes shall be at the Keil it Grapples fast to the Keil, and is wholly Disengag'd from the Machine. He then Rows off. The Powder is to be fired by a Gun Lock fixed within the Cask which is sprung by Watch work, which he can so order as to have that take place at any Distance of Time he pleases. The Experiments that has as Yet been Made are as follows. In the Most Private Manner he Conveyd it on Board a sloop In the Night and went out into the sound. He then sunk under Water, where he Continued about 45 Minutes without any Inconveniency as to Breathing. He Can Row it either Backward or forward Under water about 3 Miles an Hour, And Can steer to what Point of Compass he pleases. He Can Rise to the top of the Water at any Time when he Pleases to obtain a fresh supply of air when that is Exhausted. He has also a Machine already prepard by which he can tell the depth under water and can then admit water if it is needed to Bring the Machine into a perfect Equilibrium with the water. He has also another Pair of Oars by which he Can Rowe it either up or Down, and a forcing Pump by which he Can free himself from the Water which he Admits to bring the Machine to a Proper Equilibrium with the Water. At the Top he has a pair of Glass Eyes by which he sees Objects Under Water. These Parts are all Compleat and these Experiments he has Already Made. I might add, he has an Anchor by which he Can remain in Place to Wait for Tide Opportunity &c. and again Weigh it at Pleasure. About 1000 Weight of Lead is his Ballast, part of which is his Anchor, which he Carries on the outside at Bottom of the Machine. This story may Appear Romantic, but thus far is Compleated and All these Experiments above related has been Actually Made, He is now at New Haven with Mr. Doolittle an Ingenious Mechanic in Clocks &c. Making those Parts which Conveys the Powder, secures the same to the Bottom of the Ship, and the Watchwork which fires it. I every Minute Expect his return, when a full Tryal will be made. And Give me Leave to Say, it is all Constructed with Great simplicity, and Upon Principles of Natural Philosophy, and I Conceive is not Equall'd by any thing I ever heard of or saw, Except Dr. Franklins Electrical Experiments...

Dr. Benjamin Gale
August 7, 1775

CHAPTER 20
THE IN-SHORE SQUADRON

A few miles from the Yale campus, Washington rode his horse with Major Tallmadge following closely behind. The encampments looked more like a crowd of rabble than a proper army. But they were needed to deal with the British fleet nearby. Insects buzzed around their heads as they went to inspect the various squads of men. Washington observed bleakly that the men were poorly equipped with enough powder and shot for three volleys. After that, they would be virtually unarmed. They continued their rounds until they reached the final encampment. This time the men, who had been merchant seamen by the cut of their clothes, were straining their vision on the crest of a hill to see the drama unfold below.

"God's teeth, that's a brave one," commented a lieutenant looking through a glass.

Washington and Tallmadge quickly dismounted and walked to the group. The lieutenant was somewhat startled as Washington suddenly appeared and quickly called his men to attention where they stood.

"As you were. Please tell me what's happening."

The lieutenant, obviously a landsman, turned to a seaman to help communicate the action happening in the channel below.

"Sir, Yankee merchantmen's turned to and hauled up the channel; 'pears to be mak'in a run for our position, but the in-shore squadron's hot on it, sir. Betwixt them and the field pieces them British's got at Dorchester Heights, I don't think she's got a chance in heaven, sir."

As they looked on, the slaughter began to unfold. The Yankee schooner was trying to make a run for it past two double-deckers who delivered devastating broadsides. The little ship managed to survive two rounds of fire, but started to lose parts of the ship. As Washington listened, the sailors bantered various observations among themselves as they watched the destruction. He heard things like "she's trying heave to…beating to port… scuppers are overflowing." It was ugly as the valiant little vessel tried to go past Lechmere Point on route to Cobble Hill. But, in the end, it was no match for the fourth rates and field artillery pieces on Dorchester Heights. Even without knowledge of ships, Washington could see that the battle was lost. Even the sailors fell silent as a mass of rigging, masts, and men fell into the water only to be executed by marine sharpshooters on the yardarms of the British frigates. Some of the men may have even been their shipmates at some point in the past.

Washington walked back to his horse. He knew better than to try to say anything. His silence was more of a testimonial to their bravery than any cheap words of consolation. As they silently rode back, Washington felt sick. It was one thing to lose people in battle, another to stand by powerless. If Dorchester Heights had remained in colonial hands, he might have protected the ship with his field pieces. There must be something he could do to lend service to the Yankee merchantmen, even if just putting the in-shore squadron out to sea a couple more miles. Washington had to get more information on their operations and knew there was only one place to turn, the Culpers.

CHAPTER 21
BUNDLING

A week later, the hidden images slowly began to appear on the ragged parchment as Tallmadge, aka Culper Junior, and the lady known only as Agent 355 squinted to see more clearly. He applied the sacred reanimater to the invisible ink to reveal the message on the back of what appeared to be just a standard manifest.

Any observer would have assumed the two people were worshipping in the recessed corner of the church, where hundreds of votive candles were dotted throughout for those wishing to light a flame to signify a special prayer. The effect was the projection of dancing shadows reflected from statues on the ceiling. As a Quaker, Tallmadge didn't frequent Papist churches, but it proved the most convenient place to be seen at night without fear of reprisal.

"So, the general needs more information on the in-shore squadron?" she observed.

"Do you have any contacts we can use?" asked Tallmadge.

"I know a lady friend of Edward Thornbrough of the HMS *Falcon*."

"How close are they?"

"As close as required. She normally only considers somebody of a flag rank or other major official, but she made an exception for looks," she said, indicating a lady friend of high social standing. In the Americas and Europe, many aristocratic couples were comprised of older men with relatively younger partners. Aristocratic men didn't have the means to marry until after assuming the family holdings from an aging parent. At that time, they were seen as suitable for cementing a social/business arrangement with a leading family through marriage—including the payment of a bride's dowry. Eventually, these women, married to elderly men, sought companionship elsewhere.

Intimate relationships outside of marriage were also common in the American Colonies at all social levels. Beginning at the lowest, women often married seamen before those men left on dangerous voyages spanning two years or more, such as those in the China tea trade or whalers. During these years, women had little or no income and were often unaware if their husband would return alive. Many worked for meager wages as domestic help or seamstresses unable to earn a sufficient income to pay their bills and feed children. As a result, financial assistance often came from sexual favors to an employer, "sugar daddy," or casual encounters with others. So, prostitution was acknowledged as a part-time necessity.

Intimate relationships for nonfinancial reasons were just as common. In the respectable courting practice of "bundling," couples slept in the same bed for an evening prior to marriage to ensure compatibility. A board would be placed down the middle, or the male participant wrapped in blankets (sometimes sewn together in a bag) to be close, without actual intercourse. More often than not, the board or blankets disappeared and a pregnancy quickly followed. The bundling practice was expanded to non-courting individuals such as an employer and a domestic servant to save on wood and coal. This practice, seen as thrifty, often ended in the same result.

In the end, marriage had little to do with love, and intimacy available to many—including British officers. With this intimacy came needed information for the Patriots.

"Do you think she could be trusted to help us?" asked Culper Junior. Often these arrangements ended in the parties actually falling in love with unpredictable results.

"Yes. She has no feelings for him; he's just a source of physical attention."

As Culper Junior gazed in her eyes, he certainly understood the physical need. However, the female informant remaining out of love with the British officer was another matter.

CHAPTER 22
CAN'T SEE UNDER WATER

It had been two months since the *Turtle* was demonstrated for Dr. Gale, and winter was setting in. David and Ezra worked to perfect the machine but problems continued to occur, from mechanical failures to leaks. Now during yet another test, David was getting worried; Ezra had been below the surface almost half an hour now. He had no rigging attached to the *Turtle* because there was no one to pull it up. Besides, it kept him from steering longer courses and going deeper.

The problem that David feared most had come to pass. In the winter, with frost coming and going with changes in temperature, the foxwood he used for light inside the *Turtle* was failing. The phosphorus fungus in the foxwood ceased to produce light in the cold. It was the only element that could be found to illuminate the points on the compass and the inside of the *Turtle* in the underwater darkness.

Finally reaching the surface, Ezra swung open the hatch. It was a horrifying experience.

After a few more minutes, relief turned to anger and frustration. They had been delayed by ice in the river, a ballast pump not operating according to its design, and having to work at night due to fear of Tory informants. News of the work being whispered in the Continental Congress only added to the stress level.

When winter began, he started to notice that light-producing properties of foxwood would eventually disappear in the cold and frost. He had asked Dr. Gale to follow up with Benjamin Franklin, to find an alternate source of light. Since burning candles needed oxygen, he needed something else. Perhaps, he wrote, electricity could provide the answer. He had received no reply, because Franklin had none to give. He was on the right track, but Thomas Edison wouldn't invent a reliable light bulb for another century.

Ezra cranked the machine back to the island. It was time to ask again.

David sat in the parlor of Dr. Gale's home. The doctor was keenly interested in all aspects of the *Turtle* and kept the Continental Congress informed of progress. So it wasn't unusual for David to share the malfunctions of the *Turtle* with him.

"….now the foxwood, that's the situation, Dr. Gale. I need light."

"There are no other sources found in nature other than foxwood?"

"No, sir. I've looked. There are none. My only hope is for another source. The only thing I can think of is that Mr. Franklin's electrical experiments may lead to the creation of light." Everyone knew that electricity was found in lightning as demonstrated by Mr. Franklin's famous kite experiment. Since lightning produced light, electricity must also.

"I don't think that will solve the issue, David. However, I know that Mr. Franklin has conducted experiments on certain glowing fungi and mushrooms. Perhaps the answer lies there."

"Perhaps so, sir."

Dr. Gale sighed and moved to his writing table. "I know you've been trying, David. You're a mechanical genius, I've no doubt. But it seems like when I get an inquiry from some congressional committee about the machine, I have to report back, through Mr. Franklin, some obstacle. Even though I understand that an achievement such as yours is expected to have problems, Congress cannot seem to grasp it. As a result, some have come to mock your efforts. Therefore, I'll give an accounting of the situation and implore Mr. Deane to press Mr. Franklin for a response."

"Thank you, sir," said David. "You know how much I appreciate your help."

Gale just nodded from his writing table with a pen poised to begin yet another letter. Perhaps Congressman Deane would have some sway in getting an answer to the light problem. After a proper introduction, Gale got to the heart of the matter:

...Every trial respecting navigation answers well, but still fails on one account. Bushnell proposes going in the night, on account of safety. He always depends on foxwood which gives light in the dark, to fix points of the needle of his Compass and in his barometer, by which we may know what course to steer and the depth he is under water. Both of which are an absolute necessity for the safety of the Navigator. But he now finds that the Frost wholly destroys the quality in that wood; of which he was before ignorant, and for that reason and that alone he is obliged to desist. I write you this that you and those to whom you may have communicated what I wrote may not think I have imposed on you an idle story.

Asking for assistance in getting help from Franklin he wrote:

...Can you enquire whether he knows of any kind of Phosphorus which will give light in the dark and not consume the air? Bushnell tried a candle, but that destroys the air so fast he cannot remain under water long enough....

Dr. Benjamin Gale
December 7, 1775

Hopefully help would come soon.

CHAPTER 23
COUNTER SPY

The man, James Brattle, clutched the cloak tightly around his face as he looked at the dark street ahead. New York was a dangerous city. Not only were criminals always lurking in shadows to club a man and take his money, but with revolution in the air, you never knew who was friend or foe.

In his case, he was seen as a mild-mannered valet. He had always worked for the gentry and had begun to think of himself as such. In a strange way, devoting himself to aristocratic employers made him feel, in some way, attached to the king himself.

"You there!" called a guard posted near the entrance to a building.

"Yes," he replied confidently, in an effort to intimidate the man.

"Oh, it's you, Mr. Brattle. Out late this evening, taking care of the congressman, I see."

"Yes, always the servant."

"Well, don't let me stand in yer way, sir."

The guards stationed around government buildings and the residences of high-ranking figures knew not to antagonize their servants. It could mean instant discharge, or reassignment to a much worse post. In this case, the official was Congressman Silas Dean, a rapidly rising politician. With his zeal and charisma, he had been elected a delegate to the first Continental Congress. In his position, he knew of sensitive battle plans and correspondence with other Patriots, such as Benjamin Franklin.

Brattle was in his employ as a personal servant. As Deane's assistant, he cared for all his needs, from dressing him to assisting with his correspondence. There would hardly be a better place for a British spy. In this case, Deane had received a letter from Dr. Gale in an effort to reach Benjamin Franklin about help with some ingenious Yankee water machine.

Brattle continued down the street trying to make himself look inconspicuous. It wasn't exactly easy, in the street that included sailors and young men making merry and, of course, prostitutes. He looked slightly out of place at this hour, but it was only now that he could get away from his employer, who was fast asleep.

He would have left sooner after his master retired to bed, but he had to take the time to encode a message to New York's Royal Governor Tryon. Like other officials of the Crown, Governor Tryon had fled the city, but not before making arrangements with his spy network to keep information flowing.

Brattle finally made it to the wharfs, where an eerie fog floated along the docks. That wasn't unusual; he just seemed jittery because of his mission. He reached a prearranged drop-off point and left a simple marker. It would be completely unnoticed by any other passerby, but in this case it was a signal for a boatman to retrieve a message. Seeing the boat approach, he scurried away to avoid anything that might tip off the Patriots to his real mission.

The boatman casually arrived on the wharf and retrieved the bottle near the marker. He knew he had to bring this to Governor Tryon, now aboard a British merchantman, *Duchess of Gordon*.

After making his way across the harbor with his crew rowing against the light waves, the boatman climbed aboard the ship and approached the aft cabin, where he knocked on the door with two quick raps, followed by two more.

The governor rose from his bed. Normally he wouldn't be disturbed at this hour. But in this case, one of his spies was reporting vital news.

"Who delivered it?" he said to the rough, overweight boatman who looked as unkempt as any waterfront hooligan.

"Brattle."

"Brattle. So the Continental congressman has some tasty bit he's let out again."

"I'll be off then, sir." With a tip of his hand in a makeshift, sloppy salute, he was gone.

Tryon went back into his cabin and turned up his gas lamp. He was eager to decipher Brattle's message. Not only was it generally inside information, but also entertaining with his sarcastic view of the Americans leaking the information. After painstakingly deciphering the message by removing the appropriate words, he finally had a complete letter.

The great news of the day with us is now to Destroy the Navy. A certain Mr. Bushnell has completed a machine, and has been missing four weeks, returned this day week. It is conjectured that an attempt was made on the Asia but proved unsuccessful—Returned to New Haven in order to get a pump of a new Construction which will soon be completed—When you may expect to see the Ships in Smoke.

As is often the case with espionage, the message was predominantly wrong. Brattle had combined contents of the letter with scuttlebutt from another source. However, it was timely, being only eight days since Dr. Gale had drafted a letter. David had not made an attempt on a British ship, and Tryon had no understanding of the nature of the machine. He sat and pondered the secret information. In any case, he needed to deliver it to Vice Admiral Molyneux Shuldham. Maybe the admiral could make sense of it. He quickly called a boatswain's mate to drop a cutter.

CHAPTER 24
NEWS OF A WATER MACHINE

Townsend, alias Culper Junior, stood outside a Quaker meeting house. This would normally be a place of solace for a man like himself, but even his faith had been drawn into the conflict. As a Quaker he was bound to pacifism, with violence strictly prohibited. However, a pamphlet came into his possession from Thomas Paine entitled *Common Sense*. In it, Paine argued that Quakers were obliged by their faith to struggle against corruption and narcissism—with resistance as the means to achieve those goals. He further argued that the Quaker pacifists-at-any-price were not authentic to these ideals. Culper Junior was moved by the argument, which ultimately placed him outside the meeting house waiting for Agent 355.

It was the perfect place to meet during the day. He was a well-known Quaker and their meeting there would not be seen as out of place. In fact, it would be assumed that they were intent on worship. As he looked down the busy lane, Townsend saw Agent 355. She was beautiful by any account. Her auburn hair visible under her bonnet shined with the hint of a slight curl. Her affable personality only added to the attraction. But she was the romantic target of other men including Major John Andre, the British spymaster. So, Townsend kept his romantic interest to himself.

"Let us sit," smiled Townsend, gesturing to a nearby bench.

"I have news from Major Andre. But it seems nonsensical," she whispered with a guarded tone.

"Oh?" inquired Townsend. The agent's reports were normally concise.

"Major Andre has received word that the Patriots have developed a water machine," she said, engaging his eyes through a soft stare.

"What sort of water machine?"

"They have acquired correspondence between delegates that say a Yankee inventor has created an underwater boat of sorts—capable of attaching a bomb to the hull of a warship."

"Surely it cannot be so, just another rumor," countered Townsend. They had certainly heard their share. Much of their role seemed dedicated to separating fact from fiction in conversations. This, however, was certainly the most fanciful.

"I thought so too. However, it seems to have come from official correspondence, and the British certainly think it plausible. Apparently, it has been tested and has the backing of the Continental Congress," she shrugged.

"Do we know any British plans for defense?"

"We don't. It appears that that while many feel it plausible, others believe it to be a Yankee yarn contrived to make the fleet move farther out to sea. The group believing it to be a yarn are having their way at the moment. So, they're taking no action that I'm aware of."

"Are they searching for the machine?"

"I understand that the in-shore squadron has been asked to keep a lookout for the machine. However, I don't believe they have dispatched any group to capture it. They don't seem to know its whereabouts. I'm not sure they know what to look for."

They both sat quietly as two passersby looked warily at their discussion. It was obvious that they weren't man and wife, so human nature dictated that they were there for something more unsavory than worship.

"We must be moving on," said Townsend, extending his hand to assist the lady to stand. "I'll get word to the general. However, he may think we're daft and incapable of generating reliable information in the future," he said with a chuckle.

She parted with a quick glance of her deep brown eyes and wry smile. He could see why she was so capable of extracting information. He would gladly give her everything he possessed if given half the chance.

Washington listened intently with the look of a man hearing a tall tale. "Surely this cannot be so," he said. A machine that allows a man to travel underwater under his own power for want of sails and attach a device capable of sinking a ship?"

"Dr. Benjamin Gale, winner of the Gold Medal, has seen such a machine created by a man of singular genius. Benjamin Franklin has heard details of the machine's fundamental workings and proclaimed it to be so by his own estimation," responded Tallmadge with indignation.

"How is it that Dr. Gale came to know of this machine?"

"He was asked to view the machine by the headmaster of Yale College," responded Tallmadge.

"What do we know of this Bushnell?"

"Bushnell hails from a farm in Connecticut. It is said that he has a unique temperament that comes with an extreme intellect of God's own design. However, has a brother named Ezra that acts as the machine's operator and often speaks on his behalf to those of a more common temperament."

"So, he acts as a translator of sorts?" asked a dubious Washington.

"Yes, General."

"Are they to be trusted? They could easily deliver such a device to the Crown and be well rewarded," continued a cautious Washington.

"I believe that the Bushnell family fares back generations as farmers," said Tallmadge, not accustomed to having no report to speak from.

"How is it that this Bushnell came to attend Yale College?" asked Washington, shaking his head from the apparent disconnect. It was abnormal for a simple farmer to gain admission to a prestigious college normally reserved to children of leading families or clergy. "Apparently, his father died and left him a modest parcel for land that he sold to attend school. It is said that his preparation in the prerequisite studies was completed by a local clergyman who compressed a decade of study into a single year owning to Bushnell's keen intellect."

"How old is Mr. Bushnell?" continued Washington in what seemed like an unending barrage of questions.

"He has reached the age of thirty, sir," said an almost hesitant Tallmadge, knowing that this would invoke another Washington response. However, this response was more to his liking.

"A thirty-year-old student at Yale? He is as singularly unique as his machine," marveled Washington.

"Given his invention, you would think he understands this to be the next logical step for his machine to be brought into service. Otherwise, why would he propose to use it?"

"Given that his invention combined an explosive device with a method of clandestine transport seems to indicate no other use. Besides, not bringing the machine to either side can only result in its ultimate capture for fear of the other's deployment," confirmed Tallmadge.

"Assuming that his mind works as peculiarly as we think, he will be difficult to predict," responded a wary Washington.

"There's more, General," observed Major Tallmadge.

Washington laughed. "What else could there be?"

"Culper Junior's associate, Agent 355, reports that the British in-shore squadron has been told to look for the machine." Now, he had Washington's attention.

"So, the British have heard of it and think it a credible threat?"

"Yes, General. But not credible enough to have affected their movements."

"That's unfortunate," replied a dejected Washington.

The general paced some more. "No, Major Tallmadge. I can't try some fantastic machine. I will go with the tried and true method used by the British themselves against the larger Spanish fleet at the Battle of Gravelines."

Tallmadge, like all military men, knew of the famous battle. The Spanish armada with a fleet of 130 ships sailed an army from Flanders to invade England. Their plan was to overthrow Queen Elizabeth—thereby replacing Protestantism with Catholicism. The English responded by using a fireship to scatter the Spanish fleet. It didn't hurt that the Spanish fleet was likewise overwhelmed by a storm at sea. Either way, the end result was their defeat.

Washington's intentions seemed clear; fill a boat with combustible material. There was certainly plenty of combustible materials available including pitch, pine knots, turpentine, and even barrels of tar.

Major Tallmadge stood. Recruiting people to become spies was hard enough. Now he had to find a crew willing to sail a blazing ship at a large warship. Even the most feeble-minded knew that if the fire didn't kill them, the enemy certainly would.

"Be encouraged, Major," consoled Washington. "If this doesn't work, Mr. Bushnell may yet have his day."

CHAPTER 25
WASHINGTON'S FIRESHIP

Captain Parker sat in his cabin aboard the HMS *Phoenix*. He'd normally be out for a stroll with coffee after dinner, but he was tired. It seemed like the entire month before, the Yankee rebels on the Hudson were relentless in their attempts to sink his command. If it wasn't underwater obstacles, it was intermittent bombardment by field artillery. On July 18, a typical day, they were moored a quarter mile off Staten Island, with moderate breezes and fair seas. At 2:00 p.m., he ordered that a gun be fired as a signal to the in-shore squadron that they were to unmoor. At 3:00 they weighed anchor and came to sail in company with his majesty's ship *Rose*, a schooner, the *Tryal*, and the tenders *Shuldham* and *Charlotta*. By 3:45 they were just past the Battery at Red Hook on Long Island, near Governors Island and Powlos Hook, when they came under fire from Patriot batteries. They returned fire to no effect. To end the day at 7:00, they anchored in Tapan Bay abreast of Tarry Town. In surveying the damage, the *Phoenix* received two cannon shots in the hull, one in the bowsprit and several through the netting. For the crew, one seaman and two marines were wounded. Most days in July had similar action.

A knock came at the door.

"Enter," Parker said.

"Good evening, sir," said the midshipman.

"So, what is it?" he growled.

"Several galleys downriver, sir, nothing much to speak about." Being downriver near the British positions, they would be nothing of consequence. "But upriver there's at least one vessel, looks to be a Yankee, sir, and could be supplying the rebels."

"So, I'll be up directly." It was late and the last thing he wanted was to chase any Yankee traitors. Not tonight; he wouldn't let anything get in the way of his sleep.

Captain Thomas stood silently in his boat anchored at Spuyten Duyvil Creek. In this case, he wasn't a ship captain, but a regular in the Colonial Army. Not far away on shore stood Captain Hazelwood. They'd become well acquainted while preparing for this, the launching of their secret mission. It all began when Captain Hazelwood was called down to Philadelphia to help protect colonial positions along the Hudson from British warships. Hazelwood was selected because of his special expertise in creating "fireships."

"Anything yet?" he asked Captain Thomas, who was looking downriver with a glass.

"Nope, they're just sitting pretty, no activity."

Captain Thomas was nervous. Some people considered this a suicide mission. The plan was for him to lead a small team of soldiers on two boats filled with combustibles. When they saw the *Phoenix* and any escorts downriver, they'd slip out of the shoreline and try to grapple themselves to the warships and set the boats on fire. Another rowboat would be held in the rear waiting to pick up survivors and take them back to shore.

The *Phoenix* seemed to be quietly snoozing with the gently rocking of the waves. Thomas looked down at the volunteers piled in each boat. Most didn't own shoes and their clothes were ragged from head to toe. Each had some item of military paraphernalia like a blue band on their hat or belt to give the slightest indication they were soldiers. But they were good men who'd endured incredible deprivation for the cause including near starvation. Yet, here they were, volunteering for a mission most men would consider ludicrous.

They'd picked this night for two reasons. First, Washington's intelligence said that there'd be British patrols nearby. Second, it was a moonless night and they had a chance of slipping near the warships in darkness before being spotted.

"All right, lads. Let's quietly get our oars in the water. No noise now. Start making our way to deliver our little present to the Brits. We wouldn't want to spoil the surprise."

A couple of the younger men laughed at the joke. The rest seemed too intent on what they were about to do.

Parker stood on the *Phoenix* quarterdeck looking through his glass. He didn't see any Yankee vessel. But that wasn't unexpected. In some respects, the Yankees were like ghosts in the night. They would seem to disappear in some unseen inlet and instantly merge into the forest.

"Keep a sharp eye out or I'll have your head," he announced to the watches.

"Aye, sir," said crewmen within earshot. They knew that it wasn't unusual to have everyone on short rations because the captain didn't think they were diligent enough. His second lieutenant approached. "The rebels are running off as usual, sir."

The captain chuckled to himself. This past month they hadn't seemed to be running. In fact, they seemed to attack at almost any opportunity.

"Watch for borders," said the captain.

"Sir?" said the incredulous lieutenant.

"That's what I said. In these tight waters who knows what the Yankees are up to."

"Aye, sir. A sharp lookout for borders," passed on the young officer. The captain knew they thought him too cautious, but he knew better.

Upriver, Thomas quietly directed his men to enter the river and make for the *Phoenix* and the closest escort. At first they rowed slowly, but they quickened the pace as their excitement became uncontainable. Per the plan, he made for the larger frigate while the other boat made for the escort. Within half a league, he signaled for them to stop rowing. From here on, they'd let the currents carry them silently to the warships rather than risk being heard. The men sat completely still. All were veterans of the war and were quite accustomed to being motionless. They'd spent more than one night in the wilderness quietly waiting for a British patrol or evading being spotted by Canadian scouts.

"Stand by, men." The soldiers took out their grappling hooks attached to lines and prepared to throw them on the two ships. Thomas felt as if they'd never close the gap. The waiting seemed worse than actual action. He could barely make out the dark form of the other boat and had a hard time judging the distance. The worst thing they could do was commit too early to the river's center and be smashed by the much larger warships. Then suddenly he heard the ship's bell of the *Phoenix*. The sound, clear in the darkness, was a perfect mark for its distance.

"Courage, boys," said Thomas in a whisper. "Wait for the word."

Captain Parker yawned as he looked over the side. The ship's bell signaled that it was 11 p.m. By all rights he should have been in bed right now like most of the watch, but they had to do their duty and look for the Yankee schooner. The lookouts passed the word that all was well. It looked like tonight might be quiet after all. Suddenly fire filled the sky.

"There!" yelled the lieutenant next to the captain. "Fireship!"

As Parker looked on, rebels on a small boat were throwing grappling hooks on the tender only a few half cable lengths away.

"Drum to quarters!" he yelled. The ship's boy pounded the drum while seamen appeared like mice from every hole. In an instant, gun crews were arriving at their station and seamen were climbing aloft to get underway.

The marines onboard were firing through the fire trying to rid the boat of its sailors. The Yankees continued to haul the lines, bringing the fire to the doomed ship. Fire jumped onto the tender and it ignited like a tinderbox. Most men aboard would perish in the fire or drown.

"Another ship, a cable off the port bow!" yelled a lookout.

"Port gun crew, aim and fire!" yelled Parker. It was a futile order. At half a cable and much smaller than the *Phoenix*, the vessel was much too low in the water to be hit by the cannon balls that would fly over her head.

Captain Thomas now stood as his men prepared to throw grappling hooks and draw close to the *Phoenix* when the light appeared from the port cannons, followed instantly by thunderous sounds. The balls flew over their heads, but he knew that swivel guns and marine sharpshooters would follow within seconds.

"Now men, grapple!"

At his order they threw their hooks at the port bow. He let his men pull the lines and dive into the water before lighting the fire. When he was sure they were away, he lit the tinder. Parker felt himself blown overboard with the explosion and instantly felt the grab of the current as he tried to surface and swim in the direction of the chase boat. He struggled to swim as muskets cracked and balls hit the water. He felt a sting in his back and found himself slipping below the waves. Soon, all was calm.

The British ship captain looked on in horror as flying debris from the explosion caught the foretop sail on fire. "Cut that sail away, damn it."

Seamen were instantly on the yardarms with boatswain's knives cutting furiously at the lines trying to rid the vessel of the sail.

"Sir!" yelled the lieutenant, pointing at the fireboat. Despite seamen with axes trying to cut free the grappling lines, the fireboat continued to close on the *Phoenix*, now only feet away.

"Cut our cable!" screamed the captain.

At the bow, seamen cut free the anchor line trying to free the frigate of the small boat, whose jibboom now lay over the gunwale. The *Phoenix* drifted with the current and away from the fire. The seamen continued to put out fire as debris hit the frigate and cut away burning canvas. But within ten minutes they were clear of the fireboat. They'd somehow survived another Yankee attack and avoided the fate of the tender.

CHAPTER 26
TURTLE DEBATE

Washington listened intently to the report. "So the tender was destroyed and the *Phoenix* escaped," he said. "What about Captain Thomas and his men?"

"Most were lost, General, and Captain Thomas is presumed dead. Apparently he went into the water and didn't make it to the trailing boat."

Washington shook his head. He'd lost more men to the British fleet. Without a proper navy, he was forced to try desperate attacks such as these to protect Yankee positions against their bombardment and amphibious landings.

"Still, General, we got the tender."

"The men should be commended. However, the loss is still too high. There has to be another way."

Just then, Governor Trumbull and General Putnam entered.

Washington was in no mood to deal with more generals and a politician.

"How can I help you gentlemen?" he said in shielded disgust.

"We were hoping to talk to you about the water machine," said Putnam sheepishly.

Washington returned an icy stare. He was still disappointed with the loss of so many men with the fireship and was eager for another strategy. However, he was skeptical about a water machine for several reasons, to say nothing of the fact that it was just plain weird. He had explained these same doubts to Franklin in a previous correspondence.

"This water machine might make a real difference," interjected the governor, who sensed a silent rebuff.

"Brother Jonathan, you've met this Bushnell?" said Washington, using his nickname for the governor.

"Yes, General," replied the governor. "Mr. Bushnell was presented to me by Dr. Gale to present his drawings and results of his experiments."

"And you, General Putnam?"

"Yes, General. He seems like a quiet and steady man." He quickly added, "He's of farmer stock."

"At least that's something," said Washington. "He's not an opportunist like most of the politicians I deal with daily, present company excepted."

"Have you ever seen the machine?" he asked, addressing Trumbull.

"No, sir, but Dr. Gale has witnessed its operation. He is quite emphatic that it can travel underwater, rise and descend at will, and navigate a course for almost an hour—purely underwater."

General Washington sat thinking to himself that he couldn't believe he was considering this. But why not? He had heard from many men attempting to sell their wares for the war effort, and a handsome profit for themselves. At least Bushnell had no such motives.

"So it's completely capable of doing this at night?"

"Yes, General, if the conditions are right."

Washington looked up.

Putnam quickly added, "The condition Governor Trumbull is referring to is temperature, sir. Apparently, Bushnell uses the luminous powers of foxwood to fix a course on their compass and other internal devices. Foxwood loses these properties in the frost. I'm told that Benjamin Franklin considered the problem with no success. But if the temperature stays seasonably warm, he should have no problem."

Washington looked at Putnam. It was a damn strange offer. "Let me consider it, gentlemen."

When hearing this, most men would assume the case was lost. However, Washington always thought himself a fair man. He would sincerely consider the situation, but he didn't have long to ponder.

Pressure on Washington increased in the coming weeks as Howe's 125 ships began to crowd New York Harbor after watering and resupplying at a British naval base in Canada. Even more disconcerting, he received reports that eight thousand German mercenaries were aboard. It was said that they would be paid thirty-five pounds sterling for every American they killed and twelve pounds for any they maimed.

He likewise had continuous reports of Royal Navy transports off-loading men and supplies on Staten Island. The island was primarily inhabited by Tories who were happy to supply information on American movements. Washington knew that the configuration of New York and its waterways were difficult to defend and his hold north of the city was precarious at best.

He and General Putnam went over numerous military matters including supplies, promotions, their lack of funds, terminating enlistments that might cut their army in half, and finally strategy. This wasn't new. The British complained that even though Washington's army seemed to die a slow death from lost battles and men leaving, each spring it seemed to rise from the ashes. Unlike European armies that fought grand and glorious battles followed by a negotiation of land grants or merchant trade agreements, the Americans seemed to care little of major victory. On the contrary, they seemed to constantly return to fight another day. They didn't negotiate land concessions or trade; they seemed to want it all.

Looking at the harbor and channels leading to multiple positions, Washington was continually faced with the same problem. How do you protect against the strongest navy in the world when all you have are little privateers? The British continued to move quickly to bombard his positions with horrendous broadsides, ferry supplies to troops, and move men almost instantly from one point to another. Washington had no such luxury.

Finally Washington summoned General Putnam for yet another strategy session.

"Have you thought more about the water machine of that little fellow, Bushnell?" Putnam finally asked.

"Yes, from time to time," answered Washington, not looking up from his map.

"You know, General, he might not have to actually destroy a ship. Just news of the fact that he's being launched against vessels near the shore might give us some breathing room from the fleet. Even if they stand out just a mile further, that's just that much more warning we have before they act."

Washington reflected for a moment. "Israel, do you think it moral?"

"What do you mean, General?"

"Is it moral to attack an enemy in secret? It seems ungentlemanly."

Israel Putnam reflected for a moment. "General, I think that war's a messy business. Men die. Whether they die from a scout creeping on their position in the night, a broadside of cannon shot, or a mercenary looking to be paid for their carcass like cattle, they still die. Besides, all European navies carry false flags to confuse the enemy; the British Navy even bombards civilians. Honestly, General, I think there's nothing gentlemanly about dying; you just don't want to do it."

Washington reflected. There had been a lot of death under his command. He watched more than one dying youth, crying for home, lose his life before his eyes. He wanted it to be over, too.

"All right, General Putnam. Put this Connecticut man of yours to work."

CHAPTER 27
TURTLE GOES INTO ACTION

David and Ezra crouched on the shore, peering into the darkness. Suddenly, two blurry flashes, one after the other, emerged through the mist.

"That's it, there," pointed Ezra.

The black front of their lantern clanked as David clumsily tried to flash back their response. They continued to stare into the shadows until they heard the muffled sounds of boat oars dipping into the water. Finally, the bow cut through the night. David saw a familiar face in the boat—Captain Brewster—making him a little more comfortable. Two crewman threw mooring lines to David and Ezra, who tied off the whaling sloop.

"Is it ready?" Brewster asked, stepping onto the dock.

"Yes, it's here," pointed David.

The three walked to the wagon hidden behind the brush and trees. The *Turtle* stuck out above some straw, clumsily strewn in an attempt to hide it. The camouflage had obviously fallen during the rough ride.

"It's a peculiar-looking thing, ain't it?" commented Brewster.

David was about to defend his creation when his brother lightly touched his arm. "It is. All the more reason to get it aboard before curious eyes see it."

"Aye, mate, that we'll be doing straight away."

Brewster glanced at his crew, whereupon they moved to the machine. Apparently, years together in clandestine operations had perfected silent communications between captain and crew.

David pointed to the machine. "Please be careful with the metal coming from the hull."

They looked at him as if to say, *What hull? This doesn't look like any boat we ever saw.* But with some amount of effort, they managed to maneuver it adjacent to the whaleboat. David and Ezra were told to board as the sailors quickly dropped a cargo net and swung the *Turtle* aboard.

"You gents, move over here," directed Brewster in an attempt to keep them out of the crew's workspace. They moved to the fantail near the small wheel on the aft portion of the weather deck. "We'll get underway right quick. I don't want to lose the night with the in-shore squadron filling Long Island Sound."

The crew turned to the fore rigging and the sails filled with wind. As the sloop jerked forward, David stumbled.

"Grab the taffrail there," instructed Brewster. "If things go badly and we have to run, you'll be good to remember that."

The sails were now filled and the sloop glided silently through the water.

"What now, Captain?" asked Ezra.

"We'll go as quickly and silently as possible. Luckily, the fogbank is holding and we'll use that as long as we can."

"What happens if we run into a British ship?"

"We'll have to spin on our heels and run as fast as we can."

"We'll not fight?"

Brewster laughed. "I've got two ludicrous pivot guns compared to their fifteen or more six-pounders. Even the British Revenue Cutters outgun us six to one. No, we'll make like smoke and disappear as fast as we can."

"There's Revenue Cutters here?" asked David.

"Aye. With smuggling rampant, even the treasury's navy wants any prize they can lay their hands on."

They continued in their silent run along the coast so as not to have their sails caught in the moonlight. Everyone listened intently for any sound in the fog.

"Listen," said Brewster. They heard the steady clack of capstan pawls come across the water, indicating a ship nearby.

David, like everyone else, held his breath and prayed. After a few moments, the sound faded into the night.

A loud thud and clatter came as somebody overturned a sailmaker's bench.

"Damn your eyes to hell," said Brewster in a hushed voice. The sailor quickly dropped to his knees and picked up the tools lest they make more noise.

"Ease down your helm," ordered Brewster.

"Ease down, aye," came the automatic reply. It was customary for the helmsman to repeat back any command and confirm completion.

As they continued through the darkness, the jib flapped slightly with the change, the only audible noise on the otherwise silent sloop.

"Mainsail haul," instructed Brewster.

An hour later as the fog finally ran out, they could see two frigates and a cutter in the distance, but their pursuers were too late. David and his party had already moved up Long Island Sound and were near enough to the American position to be protected by their field guns. They docked in the emerging morning light to a crowd of men wanting to see the strange device. David was shocked at the lack of secrecy. He was glad he didn't know the level of their fame before he boarded a sloop going past the British fleet.

The *Turtle* was unloaded and secured with a guard posted next to the contraption with orders from the major to "crack the heads of any soldier who goes near."

Meeting with Brigadier General Parsons, a subordinate of Putnam, David was given a briefing. Ezra stayed in a tent with what they thought was advancing camp fever. David listened intently.

"Here," pointed the general to a hand-drawn map, "two frigates are threatening to encircle our position."

"So you'll be attacked from two sides."

"That's correct," stated the general. "Each of these ships has at least sixty guns. With that kind of firepower, we'll be hell-bent to hold our own against them and a frontal assault. And with New York like it is, we can be attacked on any number of flanks. It's bad ground, Mr. Bushnell."

David contemplated the situation. It looked bleak.

"So we need you to take on one of these frigates. If you're successful, we pray that the other will withdraw and our rear positions will be protected."

"Yes, General."

"How soon can you attack?"

"Tomorrow night, General, assuming that Ezra, the pilot, has recovered."

"Did he become drunk because of the mission?" asked the general, slightly irritated.

"No, sir, camp fever."

The general instantly looked down. "Mr. Bushnell, camp fever is bad business. Men usually die. I hope this pilot isn't too close a friend of yours."

"He's my brother, sir."

The general looked stunned. "We'll hope for God's protection, sir."

With that introduction, David rushed back to the tent. Ezra was gone. A soldier said he had been moved to a hospital tent "so as he don't infect the men."

David ran toward the hospital, sporadically asking directions from surprised soldiers. He found Ezra asleep.

"How is he, Doctor?"

"He's got camp fever. He can't retain fluids."

"He'll be all right, won't he?"

"He might. I've seen men beat camp fever. But it will take weeks." David wanted to ask more questions but the doctor went to aid another physician restraining a screaming man. This was a horrible place. For months and months, David had prayed to be brought here, and to be useful. Now he just wanted to go home.

David walked out of the tent and wept. He didn't care one iota about his invention, just his brother. But like it or not, this was a war and he would be expected to find a replacement stronger than himself.

CHAPTER 28
HMS PHOENIX BREAKS RIVER DEFENSES

Townsend, alias Culper Junior, worked in his store filling supplies for a customer. It was increasingly difficult to split his focus between running a business and acting as an intelligence operative. The double life took its toll and there was no room for anything else like any social arrangement whatsoever. Nevertheless, his mind routinely wandered to Agent 355—the only thing that brought his two worlds together.

He had been waiting for her visit that might signal intelligence for the general. But more importantly, it was her presence that made it all worth it, even if they couldn't be together.

The small bell atop the shop front door rang as the door opened and she entered. The sight of her made him happy and self-conscious at the same time. Townsend hurried to finish his business and escort him hurriedly out the door. Townsend walked to the rough-strewn counter where she stood.

"How are you?" she asked.

"All right, I suppose. How are you?" was all he could muster. He wanted to say so much more, but her social station and relationships with men, both formal and informal, kept him from broaching the subject.

"I'm fine also. It's nice to see a true gentlemen," she said with a look of sadness. He could only imagine what her life could be like. She was always "looked at" because of her beauty, but never really "seen." In many ways, she was as alone as himself. "I have information," she continued. "The *Phoenix* is going to test the river defenses within a fortnight." "Why? The in-shore squadron has already lost two ships. Why send a third?" asked an incredulous Townsend. A Philadelphia carpenter, Richard Smith, had created long iron-tipped spikes capable of piercing a ship's hull. Washington had the spikes embedded in square wooden boxes constructed of logs and dropped under water by boats at night. The spikes were angled in the direction of any British ship attempting to make it up the channel out of range of Yankee shore batteries. In short, only friendly ships that knew their placement could run the gauntlet. Two ships had already been impaled on the spikes to be pulverized by Patriot fire.

"They captured a local man they think to be a river pilot."

"So, they assume he will know his way through."

They both knew that the only safe route through the underwater maze was a closely guarded secret known only to a few. However, he could be one of those few. The British were desperate to find a way to reach and capture Washington's Fort Lee, whose strategic placement would grant them full control of the waterway and the northern colonies.

"I'll get word to the general as fast as possible," Townsend assured her. They couldn't stop the *Phoenix*, but at least they could save the fort.

"I must go," she said, moving toward the door. Townsend wondered if she had any of the same inclinations as himself. But, he simply held the door as she left.

A week later, Fort Lee was pounded by the HMS *Phoenix*, which managed the gauntlet—apparently the man knew the way. But the Yankees were ready with ten-pounders from their cannonade. After an hour-long pitched battle, the *Phoenix* withdrew. However, the fact remained that the British had navigated through the water defenses. Given the difficulty and time required by the Americans to make more underwater obstacles, it was inevitable that they would be back with reinforcements. The Patriots needed another solution—and quickly.

Days later, colonial troops marched in formation. The sergeant of each platoon, comprised of three squads, walked to the left calling cadence. In front of the company of three squads marched a lieutenant. At the front of the regiment of companies marched the regimental commanders with flag bearers. Altogether, they finally assembled in an open field, forming a series of squares before the general and his staff.

Despite the pomp and circumstance, these men wore a mixture of varied clothing, most with blue and red, and carried their own packs and guns. General Parsons waited patiently until all the men were assembled. Each regiment, including the fourth, fifth, nineteenth, twentieth, and twenty-first Connecticut regiments, finally settled in position.

David felt out of place being a civilian in such a formal group. He chose therefore to stand off to the side. It also gave him some time to be by himself. He was sick with worry about Ezra and felt extremely alone. He wished he could trade everything to be back on the farm, having never heard of camp fever.

The general made a series of comments regarding the importance of discipline, the British threat, and the need for hard training. Finally, at the end of his speech, he explained the need for volunteers for a mission involving a fireship, his word for the *Turtle*. The work would be very dangerous but was badly needed to combat the British Navy in New York. "Are there any volunteers?"

David watched as three men finally walked forward with squared corners in their step as they individually marched to form a small line before the general. After obtaining the volunteers, he announced, "Dismissed."

The three volunteers remained.

The general waved David over to ask questions of the little group. Before even asking the first question, however, he suspected that the stockier sergeant would be the one.

He asked the first and second recruits where they hailed from. Each named a small community in Connecticut. They both looked like farmers, like himself. He asked if they had operated machinery before. Both stated that they had only operated plows and the like on the farm. One had a family and one did not.

Then David approached the third. "You, sir, may I inquire your name?"

"Sergeant Ezra Lee, sir."

"Where are you from, sergeant?"

"I'm from Old Lyme, Connecticut, sir."

"I know Old Lyme. I'm from Saybrook. Have you operated any machinery before?"

"No, sir, but I'm strong and have always had a good way with my arms and the like. They pretty much do what I say," he said with a smile.

"Do you have family?"

"No, sir."

"This mission may be very dangerous."

"I'm aware of that, sir. I've had some experience and held my own in battle."

David walked over to the general. "I'd like to use Sergeant Lee if I could."

The general wasn't much for keeping men from their duties. "Thank you two for coming. It makes me proud that you volunteered. However, we need the sergeant."

The two walked off looking both disappointed and relieved—disappointed that they had no chance for fame and glory from this assignment, but relieved at a chance to live. As it was often said, "Everybody wants to be a hero but nobody wants to die."

"He's all yours, Mr. Bushnell. Use his skills wisely. He's a valuable one and will sorely be missed."

"I will, General."

The general and three officers who had remained to watch the selection walked off to the general's command tent. There, they would enjoy a little brandy and discuss possible movements by the British. More likely than not, they'd discuss the latest scuttlebutt on Washington and his slim hold on the Army. Many men were constantly jockeying for his job and lobbying influential congressmen to that end. Since Congress controlled the granting of officer commissions, and even assignments, there didn't have to be a correlation between a man's abilities and his placement in key commands. More often than not, like the British Army, these key commands were awarded because of family prominence or backroom dealings. Some had already come close to supplanting the weary Washington, and others were well positioned to take over at any sign of weakness. In fact, General Parsons' superior, General Putnam, was one of those in line for Washington's job.

David checked his pockets. He had a couple coins. "Well, Ezra, that's my brother's name also. Would you like to discuss our assignment over a pint of ale?"

"Well, thank you, sir, I would."

"My name is David. Since we'll be working together for a while, we might as well call each other by our first names." Anyway, David was so accustomed to calling Ezra out of habit, having the same name would be a natural.

Later, David looked in on his brother in the hospital tent. He was as white as a sheet as he slept.

"How's he doing, Doctor?"

"I've already lost two today to camp fever. I don't want to lose him too. But he's a strong man. It will take a while, but I suspect he'll pull through."

"Thank you, Doctor."

"This damn war. We lose more men to disease than any British infantry. It's these camps full of filth and vermin. The food is no better."

David just looked at his brother. At the moment, he really didn't care about the Army; just cared about his brother. Ezra stirred at the sound of voices.

"David, is that you?"

"Yes, Ezra. It's me."

Ezra was hot with fever and had lost badly needed fluids with endless diarrhea.

"I'm sorry, David."

"No, I'm sorry, Ezra. If I hadn't got you involved in all this, you'd be safe back on the farm."

"It ain't your fault. I'd have gone off and joined anyway."

David clasped his brother's arm. It pained him more to see him like this than to watch him descend below the water in the *Turtle*.

"Did you find anyone to help you?"

"Yes, a young man named Ezra Lee. We'll use him until you get better. Just a few days I suspect," lied David.

"Yes, just a few days," responded Ezra as he fell back to sleep.

They both knew it would be much longer, or shortened by death.

David walked out to the waiting Ezra Lee, who said, "He'll be all right, sir. I've seen other men come out of it. If he ain't a drunkard, he'll be fine."

"That he's not."

David thought that his only vice was being foolhardy enough to drive a homemade submarine into a pitching ocean to attack the most powerful naval fleet on earth.

CHAPTER 29
THE BATTLE COMES CLOSER

Townsend, Alias Culper Junior, approached the wooden printing press. At seven feet tall, it resembled a wine press from whence it came. The pressman leaned over the lower surface, placing the tightly packet metal type, while an apprentice prepared the ink to a leather-covered, handheld pillow. This smooth, round pillow would be evenly rolled on the typeface before a piece of paper was laid on its surface. That complete, pressure would be applied from above by a large threaded screw.

"Can I help you, Mister Townsend?" asked the pressman, now finished with the type placement.

"Yes, I was wondering if there was any interesting news from the *Boston Gazette*, or the *Pennsylvania Journal* and the like." The *New York Gazetteer*, where Townsend acted as a reporter, followed the normal practice of reprinting articles found in other colonial newspapers given that they had no geographic reach of their own. The *Boston Gazette* was the source of many Patriot movement events like the Boston Tea Party. The *Pennsylvania Evening Post* had the notoriety of being the first to publish The Declaration of Independence. However, Culper Junior was most interested in the *Pennsylvania Journal*. This paper was the first to publish various actions by the Continental Congress. With this knowledge, Townsend would often ask for comment on a particular action from a British source. More often than not they took the bait, off the record, and responded with some upcoming British action to "show those traitors." Today, however, there was nothing forthcoming for his alter ego, Culper Junior.

"No, Mr. Townsend. There taint nothing of the like today. However, I hear tell that the In-Shore Squadron gave the Patriots a major thumping."

This news gave Townsend a sick feeling in his stomach. He was normally aware of action before it happened, but this one was a surprise.

"What was the action?" he asked with a feeble attempt at a grin to maintain his identity as a Tory reporter.

"They say the HMS *Phoenix* led two other frigates, the HMS *Rose* and HMS *Greyhound*, into Gravesend Bay. I'm told that one pulled heavy artillery on two bomb ketches [broad-hulled vessels with two masts that held heavy armament for bombardment of shore positions]." The pressman paused to point at the ink tray to keep the apprentice working rather than listening to his narrative.

"The *Phoenix*, that's Captain Parker's ship," interjected Townsend to keep the narrative alive. That knowledge wasn't particularly impressive given that Captain Parker and the *Phoenix* were now becoming local legends among Tories for leading many such raids.

"Yes, that's the bloke," he said again while being distracted by the apprentice, who seemed to be applying the ink not in a manner to his liking.

"Why all the firepower? Were they covering some landing?" pressed Townsend.

"I'll say," he confirmed, now turning his attention to Townsend. "They covered four thousand of Clinton's men who came across Denyse Point. I hear that von Donop's corps of Jaegers and Grenadiers were among them."

Townsend absorbed the news. "That will put Patriot General Parsons in a bad way," observed Townsend. It was common knowledge that Parsons was put in charge of protecting the important posts on the North Hudson River, leading to Washington's positions.

"That's the strange bugger," confirmed the pressman. General Parsons was known for unconventional thinking, which he applied to the river defenses.

"Have you heard what Cornwallis plans next?" asked Townsend, stretching for any scrap of information to determine their next move.

The pressman just shrugged in response and returned to his duties.

Townsend quietly walked away thinking that he had to find out what came next to give the Patriots a fighting chance.

Up the North River, General Parsons argued with his aides. "Why not acquire this water machine to protect the river?"

"You can't be serious, General. Most think it fantasy. When it was called up last time, it couldn't do it."

"That's only because the pilot got camp fever and they had to train another. Do we know where it is?"

"We believe it's located near the East River."

"That's right under the nose of the British. We've got to get it moved to the North River at once."

The advisers left his cabin as he set about a letter to Major General William Heath. Heath was a no-nonsense man up for any fight. He strongly opposed the evacuation of New York and wanted to fight the British, no matter the odds. Now he was in charge of the highlands where the *Turtle* would have to cross to reach the North River.

In his correspondence, General Parsons explained:

The Machine designed to attempt blowing Up the Enemy's Ships is to be transported from the East to the North River, where a Small Vessel will be wanted to transport it. I wish you to order

One for that Purpose. As all Things are now ready to make the Experiment, I wish it not be delayed. Tho' the Event is uncertain, under our present Circumstances it is certainly worth trying."

Days later, David and Ezra Lee were on a wagon that wobbled and jerked with each hole in the road. Tree branches dragged along its sides and top from the dense forest on either side and above. Ezra sat on the wagon's bench next to David. "This is almost as black as the ocean."

David reflected for a moment. He was struck by the bravery of Ezra. Who else would entrust their life to a man who claimed to create an invention that most people considered a fantasy, and then commend himself to the ocean's bottom in it?

The forest was as black as night, and there was little light above due to the foliage that spilled over the trail. Not all trails were like this, but they had to avoid any encounter from spies, patrols, or, worse yet, Canadian scouts who could slit their throats in seconds. As David peered into the forest, he conjured up images of demons of the night.

"There's a bridge ahead," said the driver quietly. Ezra climbed off the wagon and silently disappeared into the brush. He was a soldier and keen in the woods. Bridges were ideal places for ambush. Attackers could fire from both ends of the bridge, trapping an enemy inside. There was no place to run and no place to hide.

David sat straining his ears for any sounds. Within a few minutes Ezra reappeared next to the wagon as silently as he had departed. "All clear. Just a farm cat eyeing me suspiciously."

David and the driver chuckled as they got back on their way. They had quite a few more miles to travel before dark. Despite throwing hay on the *Turtle* in the back of the wagon, it still stood out like a Connecticut Yankee in King George's court. Even covered in hay, it would draw too much attention, too close to New York and scattered British patrols.

"What do you think will be our mission?" asked Ezra.

"I don't know. I've heard that two frigates have started up the North River to breach Washington's defenses. I can only assume that we're to attack one of them."

That was a sobering thought. A frigate was a powerful thing. It carried sixty guns and almost two hundred men. It was known to pulverize coastal towns into submission.

"Do the generals have that much confidence in our machine?"

"I've thought long and hard on that question, Ezra. I believe that they probably have little confidence. But their current situation makes them desperate. If we succeed, the British fleet will be forced to stand off. If we don't, they know of our existence; the ships may stand off. The generals may be thinking that either way, they gain some success."

Ezra pondered the complexity of their military and political thinking. Some days it was better to be a sergeant.

When they finally arrived, gathered soldiers met them. The rumors that the machine would arrive spread through camp like wildfire. After months of similar rumors, the machine was actually coming to their aid. David looked at the officers, most about his own age. He wished he could have a uniform to give an air of some legitimacy instead of being the strange inventor. But a commission wasn't easily obtained.

General Parsons moved through the crowd, which automatically opened a gap for the advancing general.

"David, good to see you again."

"Thank you, sir." Getting right to the point, David added, "You wouldn't happen to have any news on my brother?"

"I'm sorry, David. I don't. The wounded and sick were moved away from the front. I have no way of knowing his current state. I'm truly sorry."

David was dejected. Now he didn't even know where Ezra was. But his movement explained why he hadn't received any answers to his letters.

"That's fine, sir," said David, getting back to business. "My new pilot, Ezra Lee, has done exceptionally well. We're ready for action, at your discretion, General."

"My discretion is tomorrow."

"Tomorrow, General?" asked David, trying to elicit the logic.

"Yes," he affirmed. "We received intelligence from one of our people in New York that the HMS *Eagle* needs to be our target to stall the British advance." With that, the general led David to his tent to explain the plan.

CHAPTER 30
TURTLE ATTACKS HMS EAGLE
SEPTEMBER 6, 1776

The forty-gun frigate HMS *Eagle* tugged at her anchor cables in the changing tide. Its duty officer paced along the deck's wooden planking as he stared at the deck lanterns of other warships moored a few leagues distant. He was tired and bored. He stamped his feet lightly on the quarterdeck to stay warm. He knew not to make too much noise lest he disturb the admiral in the aft cabin below. He'd learned from experience that Admiral Howe was irritable and the source of constant complaints. What he didn't know was that the admiral's presence also made the HMS *Eagle* a target for a new water machine secretly developed by a Yankee inventor lurking nearby.

A short distance away, Brewster's whaleboat silently cut through the inlet. Unlike the king's ships, the grimy little whaler was hideous in comparison. It had no clean lines or brightly colored flags, just the well-worn sails of a working boat. However, it blended well with area vessels and looked completely harmless.

"I hardly like coming this close to the fleet's guns, Mr. Bushnell. In this close inlet, there wouldn't be much room to maneuver if they took a disliking to us."

Brewster was one for understatement. The whaler carried only two guns. They would be no match for the British nine-pounders in a fight.

"Yes, Mr. Brewster. I understand."

"Are you sure about the contraption this time?"

"Yes, Captain. If Ezra here can manage it, it will work." Brewster looked highly skeptical, having been down this road before.

Ezra and David had practiced with the *Turtle* now for several weeks in different locations. Ezra Lee was becoming more accomplished an operator.

The word was given and the foremast jacks steadied the *Turtle* while Ezra turned to David for last-minute instructions. They were silent despite the men anxiously waiting. Finally David said quietly, "You're in God's hands now, Mr. Lee."

There was nothing more to say. He had either gained enough proficiency to drive the craft or he hadn't. More importantly, a million things outside his control could go wrong. The finicky ballast pump could fail; waves could overcome the tiny craft; a sharp thinking lookout could spot the odd-shaped round ball and drum to quarters, quickly followed by ball and shot. His life was truly in God's hands.

Ezra clambered onto the *Turtle*. Steadying himself with his foot at the opening, he managed to drop in without capsizing. He gave the signal to the whalers, who began to row toward the fleet.

One of the whalers whispered in a husky voice, "Yer ready, mate?"

"Aye, aye," responded Ezra a few feet from the boat. With that, he let go the line and the *Turtle* floated astern.

"Keep your wits about you. We'll be back to retrieve you when you're done. The *Eagle* is dead ahead," said the boat coxswain with an artificial smile. He probably didn't believe that Ezra would survive long enough to be picked up, but wanted to instill confidence. Two other crewmen waved to show their support. Ezra thought whalers or not, they're as good as men you'd find in any infantry line.

Ezra began to hand-crank the propeller. Before long, he was moving at three knots. At this rate, it would take about half an hour to reach the *Eagle*. With its black, round hull, it fit easily into the surrounding sea. He wouldn't have to submerge until he made about half the distance. As he cranked away, the physical exertion took away some of his nervousness.

As he continued, he could make out the closed gun ports of the *Eagle*. That meant that a lookout could possibly spot him. He breathed out slowly and took in a long breath. This was the last bit of fresh air he'd probably have in a while, maybe ever. He reached up and closed the hatch. It instantly became as dark as a coffin. Only the foxwood glow and some little light showed through the glass eyes. Reaching down, he felt for the ballast valve and closely watched the cork in the depth gauge move as the little boat descended. Seeing it drop he quickly closed the valve and waited for the *Turtle* to stabilize. The cork seemed to stop. He was now fully committed.

He continued to crank the propeller as the *Turtle* moved forward. He began to turn and used the rudder to try and move it back on course. It was even darker now as the lights of the windows were replaced by the blackness of the night's ocean. Only the little glow of the foxwood showed the faint outline of the compass, depth gauge, and his hands as they touched the devices. The air was becoming dank now. He was too low to try and use the snorkel to replenish air and too near to the boat to come nearer the surface. His limbs were becoming tired from the warm, used air of the *Turtle* and the physical exertion of cranking the steel propeller. He was beginning to wonder if he was even near the ship or if he should turn around and try another night. Finally the faint glow of the ship's lights appeared through the distorted images of seawater. They became clearer as he came closer to the ship. He stopped cranking to push his face against the eyes in an effort to see upward. He could tell he was close now.

He could hear his short and shallow breath in the stale air. His heart was racing, partly from the physical exertion, partly from trying to command his discipline and fight the urge to flee to the surface. His eyes stung from salty sweat coming into his eyes. He hurriedly wiped his forehead. Now it was time for the more difficult part, if that was possible.

He felt for the ballast valve and dropped the *Turtle* about ten more feet in the water, as best as he could estimate. He turned the hand crank slowly and moved forward, trying to make silent contact with the bottom hull. Now he was holding his breath, waiting for a thud. Seconds turned to minutes...nothing.

He pushed his face against the glass and couldn't see the lights, only darkness. He could have missed the hull entirely, he thought. He twisted his spine to push his face against the glass behind his head. There was some faint light above. Yes, he had missed it.

He turned the rudder and tried to make a small turn to redirect the *Turtle*. As he pushed his face against the glass again, the faint lights were now in front. Focusing his eyes as best he could with the slight glow of the foxwood on the floating cork, he felt for the ballast pump and watched it slowly rise. Each minute, the rise in the cork made him want to stop. Any second he could rise too high and be seen through the water by a lookout. But he had to get it right this time. As it rose, he stopped pumping.

Now he began his slow crank of the propeller again, holding his breath until he could feel the thud of the hull. First ten seconds, then twenty seconds. He was almost convinced that he'd missed again, and then his forward motion was stopped with what seemed like a thunderous thud. He held his breath again, waiting to hear the sounds of a mustered crew or musket fire...nothing.

He reached for the hand crank near his head to begin drilling a hole in the wood hull. As he contorted his body to get leverage, still nothing seemed to happen. He cranked and cranked, but could feel no movement.

"Why won't this go in?" he said in panic. Then he had a flash: he must have hit an iron banking on the keel. Ezra was sorely dejected. It took him too long already to get this far. The air was hot and stale and he was already beginning to have difficulty seeing. The glass was beginning to be covered with the fog from his breath. He had no choice. He had to try and maneuver once again. He would have to move to a different spot and move higher on the hull to find clear wood.

He moved the top propeller to drop down just slightly and turned the propeller crank again. He tried to use his other hand to move the rudder while he quickly reached down to expel water with the ballast pump. In the process he tried to focus his now hazy mind on the almost indiscernible cork on the depth gauge. He could barely see it and it didn't seem to move. Was the ballast pump failing?

Just then he focused on the cork that was racing to the top. He immediately stopped pumping but it was too late. The *Turtle* burst through the surface right next to the ship.

Ezra held his breath wondering if the watch heard the *Turtle* or saw its top above the water. His first urge was to open the top and flee, swimming below the ship while they shot at the *Turtle*. But he quickly regained his senses, reached down to the now visible ballast valve, and let water in to quickly submerge. He sat silently below the surface, waiting to hear the gunfire.

Seconds turned to minutes and the gunfire didn't come. As unimaginable as it was, the lookouts didn't see or hear the *Turtle*. They were too accustomed to looking in the distance for enemy sail that signaled the approach of a small boat. They never thought to look over the side.

But now Ezra could see that the night sky was fading to the glint light of a morning sunrise. That in combination with his physical exhaustion and lack of air made him consider his options. Do I stay and try again, or begin my travel back to try again another day? After thinking a moment, Ezra realized that the morning light was advancing to the point that he would be seen trying to escape, even if he were successful, which in itself was doubtful. The morning light also brought an increased chance of being seen by seamen who would soon be coming on deck to replace the night's watch.

He began hand-cranking the propeller and turned the rudder once again to get distance from the ships. He failed, and his life was still in great jeopardy as the air diminished and his arms became too weak to crank the propeller. He began his lonely trek underwater back out to an open channel in hopes of escaping and getting picked up by the whaleboat. If not the whaleboat, at least he could try for the marshy shore.

The air was foul now and he needed to surface. He was probably too close but feared that he'd pass out at any moment. Reaching down now, almost in a daze, he felt the ballast pump and began pumping the water out. Now that there was sufficient light from the morning sun, he could see the *Turtle* rise. Within seconds it broke the surface. He reached up and flung open the hatch, thrusting out his head and gasping for air. The brisk air felt as sweet as honey. He looked around and saw that he was well away from the ships. In the process of navigating he noticed that the compass wasn't working. He submerged again, surfacing every few minutes to confirm that he was sailing in the right direction. Unfortunately, his strange zigzagging motion and constant surfacing threatened to rouse the suspicion of soldiers at Governors Island.

He was now within easy sight of one end of an embankment with a soldier patrolling.

He turned the rudder and started making his way away from the island. Hopefully they wouldn't see him. He knew he should submerge again but was too exhausted to try. As it was, even with fresh air, he could barely crank the propeller with his aching, numb muscles. At least the waves were increasing in size a little to cover his actions while in a trough.

He turned his head to look at the fort and saw two sentries walking along the battery of guns. At first they just seemed to go sleepily about their business. He tried to crank away but the current kept pushing him toward the island.

Just as he considered his predicament, things got terribly worse. One of the sentries pointed at him in the distance and seemed to beckon the other guard. Soon, an officer was standing beside them with a field glass. They had spotted him.

Before he knew it, almost the entire contingent of four hundred soldiers stationed at Governors Island could be alerted to his presence and placed at the ready. He continued to crank the propeller away as fast as he could.

Are they going to try cannon shot? he thought. At least I will be hard to hit and they'll have to work at it.

As he watched, the officer seemed to direct the guard who ran. What was he doing?

Ezra quickened his pace in his effort to flee from the island. Even with the current, he was over two knots. As he looked back five soldiers ran along the shore and climbed into a boat. That's it, he thought, they're going to come after me and shoot me down.

Four soldiers climbed in the boat and took up positions at the oars. The fifth waited until they were in position and quickly cast off. They quickly made for Ezra.

"Damn!" He had no rifle, no pistol, not even a saber. Then he looked at the magazine bomb intended for the ship. Its large protrusion had been a drag on the otherwise sleek, round *Turtle*. Releasing it should help him move away faster and, with luck, might even destroy the boat.

He quickly used the trigger mechanism to start the timer. He had no forward motion now as he tried to maneuver the *Turtle* to release the powder-filled magazine in their direction. As he watched, he could now make out the determined features of the man at the tiller.

"Damn, they're fast." They were now already within fifty yards and he released the magazine. With a click, it dropped from the *Turtle* and floated in their direction. He hadn't had enough time to properly calculate the timer.

Ezra turned and cranked as fast as he could to evade his pursuers. He could see them begin to load muskets when one pointed to the floating magazine, now for all practical purposes, a mine.

They seemed to have some hurried discussion when suddenly they turned away. They must have suspected that the keg was dangerous and decided their prey in the one-man contraption was no great military threat, just an odd curiosity.

"Thank God!"

Ezra, near total exhaustion, kept cranking the propeller. He was trying to make for anything except the island or the fleet. Perhaps a passing boat would pick him up thinking he'd somehow gone adrift.

In the distance, he could make out what appeared now to be the whaler.

He waved his arms, hoping to get their attention, and watched as a whaleboat came from around the seaward side. Ezra stopped cranking and tried to get the cramps out of his arms from cranking and legs from sitting crouched for hours. As he tried to stand as best as he could, the boat appeared to steer for him.

He thought of waving again but didn't want to draw even more attention from the island. Finally as the boat neared, he recognized the men from the whaleboat. The forward-most hand stood to throw a line, and he quickly moved to tie it off. Ezra just slumped in the *Turtle* and closed his eyes. The whaleboat quickly tacked back while he enjoyed forward motion generated from something other than his own muscles for a change.

Now a safe distance from Governors Island, the crew dragged the incapacitated Ezra up and onto the deck.

Ezra took a long drink of water handed him by David. I really needed that."

"You did fine work today," affirmed David.

"I didn't sink anything."

"That doesn't matter. We can think about that later."

They sat silently for a moment before Ezra started to recount the story, focusing on his attempt to attach the bomb.

David listened intently. "So, a steel bar was in the way?"

"Yes, betwixt the rudder hinge and the ship's hind quarter."

"Too bad it wasn't copper sheeting. We could have pierced that. Then what happened?"

Ezra went on to describe his rapid ascent to the surface and race to dive, "like a porpoise." He went on to explain how he thought the "moon was only two hours high" and the morning sun would soon be arriving with boats zigzagging the harbor in their normal duties. So he would start his journey back and keep their vessel secret for another day.

"You did exactly the right thing, Ezra. There'll be another day."

As they chatted further they heard an explosion. Turning their heads impulsively to the direction whence it came, they saw the remnants of a mountain of sea spray descending from its source. The powder magazine timer had finally gone off, attracting the attention of every ship in the harbor. From their vantage point, they could hear drummers on each British ship of the line and frigate call their crews to battle stations. Cannons would be run out and men put aloft while the lieutenants and captains alike tried to figure out what happened.

"There goes our little secret," said Ezra. "At least we know it works. Look at the force of that explosion."

David reflected. "Yes, but it won't take long for the British to put the pieces together and be on the lookout for our machine next time."

The normally gruff Brewster came their way. "Well, congratulations, gentlemen." At first David recoiled from the perceived insult.

"No, I mean it. That damned thing really put a hole in the ocean. If a ship was above it, it would surely been ablaze by now. It worked. I look forward to reporting back to General Washington."

David just nodded and said, "Thank you." At least this was a small consolation. The usual jeering he got about the *Turtle* might at least command some small respect now.

CHAPTER 31
NEW YANKEE THREAT

"Them young skippers are about to get an earful from the old man [the admiral]," mused an old seaman from the wharf while looking out at the in-shore squadron.

Townsend, alias Culper Junior, saw the signal flags hoisted above the HMS *Eagle*, which seemed to trigger the launching of smartly dressed boat crews from each warship in the harbor.

"What happened?" he asked. Townsend found that waterfront seamen were often more reliable than any officer in knowing the comings and goings of the fleet. They could rely on what they saw in the way of ship movements and preparation rather than rely on hearsay. But in this case, Townsend was after the hearsay.

"The foremast hands told me that the Yankees blew up a floating bomb near Governors Island."

"That doesn't sound important enough to cause all this commotion," observed Townsend.

"It wasn't the bomb by itself that caused such a thither. It was the craft that brought it."

Townsend knew in an instant what he meant. The strange water machine that he'd heard about from Agent 355 had to be the culprit. And unless he missed his guess, it would be the number one target of every ship of the in-shore squadron and jackleg in uniform.

In the King's Navy, being called for a meeting aboard the admiral's flagship was something to snap to about. Each ship had secured from general quarters and their boat crews changed into their best checkered shirts and white pants. Boats were quickly dropped to the side while the captain, his favorite boatswain, and in some cases another senior officer quickly rowed to the ship. As the fleet looked on, the speed of which each boat was launched and the crispness of its handling were scrutinized. They took it as a sign of how well the captain ran his ship.

The last boats hit the water with screaming captains yelling curses at their crews. Being last to drop over the side was something that wouldn't happen again next time. The seamen would be beaten as an incentive to never let it happen again.

As each boat arrived, the command was given "up oars!" by the coxswain in charge of the boat. Like their speed on entering the water, how uniformly they attended their oars while sitting at attention was appraised. A few stray oars would mean an even worse beating upon return to the ship. Each captain climbed aboard the flagship trying not to falter under the guise of countless telescopes from every ship in the harbor. Even this would be a sign of weakness. On reaching the deck, flag lieutenants would greet each captain and have their arrival piped aboard by a boatswain's whistle as an introduction. Quietly, their boats hauled off to wait for a signal to return as smartly as they came.

Finally each captain squeezed into any empty chair brought into the admiral's aft cabin. It was normally relatively spacious, but with the officers crowded inside to sit, it became cramped from corner to corner. Just hours before, the walls of the cabin had been opened to make it part of the gun deck. Aft cannons were likewise run out as the crew was drummed to quarters by a marine. Following the confusion of the *Turtle*'s bomb, the ships were secured and the walls run back into place on runners, creating the aft cabin once again.

The last captain to arrive normally brought the ire of the admiral. Never mind that their ship may have been farthest from the *Eagle*. His tardiness would be taken as a personal insult and a sign that they lacked initiative.

"Damn you, sir!" yelled the admiral at the last arriving captain. The other officers sat silently, pleased they weren't his targets on this day. "If you don't take proper care of your ship and responsibilities, I'll have your command given to someone more capable."

"I beg your pardon, Admiral," said the captain, slinking to the remaining open seat.

Any response would be a career-ending mistake. Despite their titles, most were in their twenties and thirties from prominent families like the admiral. In the Royal Navy, initiative and skill didn't necessarily mean advancement. It more depended on your family's status in social circles. As a British officer, your strategy was more often to just stay alive and avoid political mistakes.

The admiral sat behind his writing table. "Months ago, one of our spies reported to Admiral Shuldham that a Yankee traitor named Bushnell had created a water machine capable of attacking a king's ship from under water." A couple of captains laughed, thinking that the admiral was joking. His quick look of anger and piercing eyes quickly made them shrink in their seats in silence. Clearing his throat he continued. "The spy reported that he had made an attempt on the HMS *Asia*. We dismissed this as just another fanciful tale by our bumpkin Americans. But today, the machine was spotted near Governors Island. The explosion you heard was a powder magazine it carried with some timing device. Apparently it was designed to be attached to a warship from under the sea. We don't know why it was released in the channel, but as you all saw from the ferocity of the explosion, it seems a very real threat."

The room was silent as the captains all looked shocked.

Finally Captain Parker spoke. "How is it so, Admiral? Surely such a machine cannot exist." He was probably the only captain who could get away with such a question, given his almost legendary exploits against the Americans on the Hudson.

"Surely, sir, it does exist. The spy also reported that he had mastered the ability to rise and sink in the water and move in any direction he sees fit."

There was a lot more murmuring in the room. Finally, Parker continued. "What are your orders, sir?"

"Don't be thick, man!" chastised the admiral. "Double your watches and instruct them to be looking in the water below. The in-shore squadron will be actively searching for Mr. Bushnell and his little ship killer. Move your ships out further from land to guard against its launch. Dismissed!"

As the group left, the admiral was left with only his own flag captain, John Hunter. "Sir, do you think it made an attempt on the *Eagle*?"

"My choosing the *Eagle* as my flagship is well known, and the *Eagle* is one of the largest ships at harbor. Yes, I assume that we may have had a silent visit from this infernal water machine in the night."

"If this thing isn't caught, it could change things."

"What things, sir?"

"Everything."

CHAPTER 32
BUSHNELL—PUBLIC ENEMY NUMBER ONE

David and Ezra sat in Roe's tavern trying to stay out of the search path. Washington had received information from his spy network that the *Turtle* was to be the subject of searches by every able-bodied solder available. As a result, the *Turtle* was well hidden. Oddly enough, the strategy to keep David Bushnell safe was quite the opposite. What better place for men to look inconspicuous than in a public drinking establishment.

As they sat nursing their ale, ten British solders burst inside. It was obvious that they were in no mood for merriment. They seemed more intent on drowning their sorrows.

"How far do you think we walked today?" complained one, removing his boots.

"Too far," growled his buddy, "and for what, some fairytale of a Yankee machine."

"If you ask me, it's just some story to scare off our fool admirals."

Actually, he wasn't the only person holding that same opinion. Many Tories and Patriots alike thought it just a wild story to harass the British. Some even said that the Continental Congress had a committee that created the story to make the Royal Navy waste energy chasing shadows.

"You there," continued the soldier, pointing at David and Ezra. "You two hiding some ship killer?" With that the men laughed. David tried faking a chuckle, hoping his look of horror didn't gave him away.

Soon the soldiers would be on to the second or third ale and the danger would be gone. David and Ezra tried to look relaxed until they could casually slip out of the tavern. They discussed their likelihood of being called upon for another attack.

"We'll be set to try again. The magazine explosion has given enough evidence of our success that they want to try again," said David.

"It will be harder next time."

"Yes, they'll be watching."

Just days later, the *Turtle* was towed from Connecticut up the North River to Fort Washington for another action.

Soldiers gathered to look at the strange machine. David was nervous as so many hands tried to move the appendages from the wooden hull.

"I'm sorry, please don't touch that."

"You going to launch that contraption for another attack?"

"He ain't allowed to answer that, stupid. Ain't it obvious?"

David and Ezra went back to filling the torpedo with gunpowder and affixing it gently to the *Turtle*. Finally they stopped and simply sat on the shore. The tides were violent that day.

"Do you want to wait until tomorrow?" asked David. "The tides may be better by then."

Ezra thought a moment, "No, war is fickle. You'll never find the perfect time or place to attack. I'll manage."

In the distance they saw the single sail of the boat approaching. "There it is," said Ezra, thinking aloud. His tone was ominous, almost like a man waiting for guards to take him to a gallows rising in the distance.

Finally the boat arrived as the sun fell below the horizon. They were exactly on time.

The coxswain directed the seaman to attach a line to the *Turtle*. "Lively now, we ain't got all night." They quickly obliged and the *Turtle* was now bobbing in the waves directly behind the boat. David and Ezra went to climb aboard only to be accosted by the coxswain. "I was told only one passenger," he said. "The pilot of this here water machine."

"Well, your orders were wrong. I'm going along," said David

The coxswain was about to object further when the stocky Ezra intervened in his husky voice. "The gentleman said he's coming aboard. Is that clear?"

"Yes, sir," responded the coxswain.

The long boat slid into the water. Within thirty minutes, David could see the outline of British frigates in the distance. Unlike before, they were further out to sea.

"Those frigates are standing off because of you, Mr. Bushnell," said the coxswain.

"Are they really?" David couldn't help but smile. If nothing else, the *Turtle* had an effect on the British fleet. David always knew that the *Turtle*, theoretically, should have a similar effect as sharpshooters have on the front lines of enemy troops. He had heard that even their morale is affected by the constant fear of a marksman's bullet silently delivered from a distance. At least that was some consolation.

The sailors hauled the *Turtle* next to the stern so Ezra could climb aboard. It was no easy task. But it was better than being cramped in that small vessel for longer than he had to be.

"May God protect you, Ezra" was all that David could think to say. He knew Ezra was a man of faith who believed in God's providence.

Ezra detached the line and quickly slid out to sea. His target was the HMS *Phoenix* anchored off Bloomingdale, or what would later become 110th Street. The *Phoenix* had been wreaking havoc with the colonial Hudson River defenses and was selected as their next target. After closing the lid, he began his slow descent into the blackness of the strange undersea world.

In the distance, Captain Hyde Parker Jr. silently ascended the *Phoenix* quarterdeck. He could hear the helmsman whisper "Captain's approaching" to the midshipman on watch. He laughed to himself. Every smart officer had the crew instructed to inform him when the captain approached. It was an unwritten rule in the Navy to never be caught off guard where the captain was concerned.

"Good evening, Captain," said the senior midshipman as he saluted and quickly moved to the opposite side of the *Phoenix* quarterdeck. It was customary to let the captain have his privacy.

Parker thought to himself how bored he was. They hadn't had any excitement since Sandy Hook. His mind went back to six months before. The Colonials had planned to destroy the lighthouse that guided ships to New York, rather than have it controlled by the king's men. They sent some Colonial amateur named Colonel Tupper to lead three hundred Yankee troops armed with two six-pounders to slog through the marshes on the Sandy Hook peninsula. It wasn't long before the peninsula lit up with orange and yellow flashes and crackled with musket fire. For an hour the skirmish continued. But the Yankee cannons couldn't penetrate the lighthouse's seven-foot-thick stone walls.

The Yankees held their own against the small contingent of marines holding the lighthouse. But Captain Parker wished he could have seen the rebel's eyes as the *Phoenix* arrived and brought her guns to bear on the Americans. Within minutes, the Yankees were forced to withdraw back into the mud and muck of the black marsh whence they came.

But that was then. Since that time, the *Phoenix* had been forced to fight an even more deadly foe, boredom. He walked back by the starboard watch. "Don't forget to watch the water for that Yankee machine." He was almost embarrassed to say it. But the admiral's information seemed irrefutable. They had even found some sort of watch-like timer on a piece of wood floating in the water where the bomb was released and exploded near Governors Island. No matter what they said, those Yankees were an ingenious lot.

Since that time, they had a dry run to test Fort Washington's defenses. Normally ships wouldn't dare to attack a shore position. Cannon, protected behind stone or earth, could continue to pound a ship's hull that had no such protection. However, Fort Washington was hastily constructed and of little armament. Just a few days hence, he would again attack the fort, but this time with at least one other frigate in tow.

Nearby, Ezra cranked the propeller of the *Turtle*. He could feel it jerk up and down in the underwater currents. He was afraid that the *Turtle* would begin rolling in the violent water and he'd have no more control. Like before, he was becoming tired, but he remained on the surface until he got closer to his prey. It had been at least an hour since he began his trip and he should have been seeing the light of the *Phoenix* by now.

This time, the plan was different. When close to the ship, rather than go deep into the water and attach the magazine into the keel, he was to go near the surface and attach the magazine just below the waterline. The plan was good in that it avoided another failure due to hitting iron, but bad because he had a much greater chance of being spotted by a sailor of the watch.

Finally, he could see the detail of the ship's lanterns above the water at a distance. He increased his cranking. He had to get closer.

Back on the *Phoenix*, the watch peered into the water as the captain had instructed. In the three years he'd been in the King's Service, the boatswain's mate had never heard of such a thing. He had seen good officers and bad officers alike come and go. He had always avoided the rack by being quick to oblige any order given, either from the captain or even by a twelve-year-old midshipman who had no idea about how a frigate operated.

As he looked into the water, he saw a strange black shape coming closer in the distance. He had to check his eyes. Could it be a whale this close to shore? No, it looked more like a sea turtle. He watched closely as it seemed to move slowly. My god, he thought, that's no turtle—that's huge! Now it appeared to be poking its head above water. Then he realized that it was no sea creature; it was a man. He quickly yelled, "Water vessel, ahoy!"

Parker raced to the gunwale and peered over the side to see the object, now almost in contact with the hull. He grabbed the first marines to appear on deck and yelled, "Fire!"

Ezra heard shots and saw tiny water spouts form as musket balls hit the water. He slammed the hatch closed and reached down into the black floor of the *Turtle*. Where's the valve? He felt the coldness of the valve metal and let water in as fast as he could. The *Turtle* began to race to the bottom. In the blackness and his panic, he couldn't see the cork on the depth gauge with the little glow provided by the foxwood. The *Turtle* seemed to creak and cry in pain from the pressure of the tons of seawater bearing down upon it at this depth. Water was seeping in through the cracks and accumulating by his feet. The *Turtle* was dying.

He used all his strength to crank the propeller and attempt his escape.

On the surface, Captain Parker had to move fast. Turning to his first lieutenant he ordered, "Get us underway, now!"

"What direction, sir?"

"Any direction—just get us moving."

The deck was now a flurry of activity. Sailors ran up the shroud and loosed sail. Other men cranked on the anchor chain to loosen the ship. Within minutes, the *Phoenix* grudgingly lumbered forward.

Each officer was now peering through telescopes through gun ports to spot the Yankee machine. Parker himself wildly scanned the surface for any sign of his attacker.

"Damned, that infernal machine," he swore. In the past, naval warfare could see the enemy miles in advance. They had time to try and maneuver in an attempt to obtain the wind gauge to attack their enemy with swivel guns or broadsides. Even if the enemy was able to close, they had time to prepare the crew to fight off borders that swung aboard.

This was totally different. They were now afraid of one little machine that had the ability to sneak up undetected and sink the ship without providing any warning at all.

"Look out there," he said, yelling to the crow's nest. "Do you see anything?"

The lookout stammered from the spars above, "No, sir."

The captain realized that the lookout probably had no idea what to look for. This was a whole new kind of enemy.

Thirty minutes had passed as morning light began to illuminate the area. Ezra, now on the surface, could see the nearby *Phoenix* in the emerging light. He fought exhaustion and the current as best he could and made his way up the harbor and away from the frigate.

Seeing his pursuer, Ezra closed the hatch and let in water once again. He would move below the surface to evade the *Phoenix*'s gaze. But in the rough currents, control was difficult with little forward progress. The frigate would quickly arrive at his position and bombard him with cannon shot until one finally destroyed the *Turtle*.

Ezra thought as quickly as he could. If he stayed here, the frigate would eventually find and sink him. If he went to shore, the marines would target him from the top masts. Seeing the water through the *Turtle*'s eyes, he realized he'd rather die like a soldier on the beach than suck water in his lungs at the bottom of the sea. He headed for the shoreline.

The *Phoenix* topmast man shouted to the officer below, "Machine ahoy!"

Captain Parker looked in the foremast shrouds to see the seaman pointing to starboard. Raising his glass he searched the surface. He saw the machine in the process of closing its top hatch to descend below the surface.

"To the starboard battery!" yelled the captain. "Lively now, lads."

The gun crews rushed to their positions. The ship's boys ran powder and shot to each cannon.

"Get marines aloft."

Marines scurried up to take positions in the rigging. From this vantage point, they could get an angle on the *Turtle*.

The lieutenant reported that each deck was ready.

"Very well, fire as you bear."

With this order each gun crew was supposed to fire as they saw the enemy. Traditionally, that was easy. They would shoot at the ship that lay hundreds of yards, or less, away. The *Turtle* was something else. Gun captains leaned over cannons to try and catch a glimpse of the *Turtle*. With a jolt and the huge bellow of cannon, smoke erupted from the hatches. Cannon shot landed all around the last position of the machine. "Keep firing as you bare!" shouted the captain.

In the end, most just gave up and fired indiscriminately. This would become a standard in anti-submarine warfare for years to come.

The little *Turtle* pitched and rolled with each explosion, the sound deafening. Each time a cannon ball hit the water, the *Turtle* seemed to jump sideways in the water.

"Damn!" exclaimed Ezra.

Realizing that he had only minutes to live, Ezra made for the surface to abandon the *Turtle*. Furiously pumping out the water with the ballast pump, the *Turtle* broke through the canopy of water. He flung open the hatch and saw the shore about fifty yards distant. Another ball struck now just short of the little machine. Ezra scrambled over the side and swam for his life.

CHAPTER 33
GOOD-BYE TO THE TURTLE

David and Ezra Lee stood in front of General Washington. It was a bittersweet ending to the *Turtle*, but at least Ezra had reached the shore and escaped very much alive. David had always imagined that they'd be toasting their success at the sinking of a ship and the withdrawal of the fleet to a safer distance. Maybe even jointly planning their next attacks. But this was altogether different, with David pleading his case before the general.

"The *Turtle* can be raised. With a few modifications, I'm sure I could…"

General Washington held up his hand to stop David. "Mr. Bushnell, you're a mechanical genius, I have no doubt. However, I've also no doubt that a combination of too many things are requisite for the success of your machine. Try to understand that a cannon, or rifle, can be operated by a Colonial regular in the worst of conditions. Their simplicity and rugged nature make it so. But the operator of your machine requires the right set of conditions from currents to underwater objects, not to mention the inherent complexity of operating such a novel device in battle. I fear that now that the British are ever on their guard to watch for your machine, your task is that much more difficult."

"But, sir," interjected David.

"I'm sorry, Mr. Bushnell. But it's entirely too dangerous. With every British ship in the squadron vigilantly watching for any underwater aberration, it would be suicidal. But don't take this as an admonition of failure in any degree. Everyone must concede that the British fleet is now standing further off shore. For that, you have succeeded where our shore batteries have failed. For that alone, you are to be commended. Further, I'm impressed enough with you and your work to requisition funds to further your efforts with the waterproof magazine and powder. I'm convinced that if another way is found to deliver it to a vessel and attach it to the hull, you'll enjoy success."

General Washington rose as a sign to leave.

David was obviously disappointed, but it was clear that the *Turtle*'s role was now complete. His disappointment was tempered by the realization that it was now too dangerous for Ezra Lee.

The pair departed, accompanied by General Putnam and Governor Trumbull.

The general was the first to speak. "David, the general is right. You and Ezra have done amazing work. Don't be disheartened."

David straightened. "Yes, thank you, General. Of course I appreciate all the support that you and Governor Trumbull have provided and will always be grateful. None more so than having provided the services of Sergeant Lee."

David turned to Ezra and extended his hand. Ezra smiled and returned the handshake. "It was an honor, sir."

"What will become of the sergeant now?" asked the governor, turning to General Putnam.

"We have special plans for Sergeant Lee. He's far too valuable to waste, to be sure."

"David, we'll discuss plans tomorrow. For now, get your affairs in order." This seemed to be a signal to take their leave and say what would only be tearful good-byes for the two men.

As they now stood alone, David hugged the burly sergeant. "Ezra, what can I say? I wish I could have offered you the fame and glory that you deserve. I'm sure you'll find that success elsewhere. You're a man of singular quality."

"And you likewise, Mr. Bushnell, with the addition of one of the greatest minds of our time. But what of your brother? Have you still heard nothing?"

"No, I'm afraid. I think I'll take this time to do a diligent search for him and his condition."

"Well, by God's grace, I pray that you'll find him well, sir."

With that, they departed to go their uncertain ways. But, David didn't have long to wait. General Washington did indeed have plans for his torpedo as a water defense and would soon put David to work.

CHAPTER 34
BRITISH GAIN A PRIZE

Tallmadge, just returning from the newspaper where he attempted to gain information for his alter ego Culper Junior, saw Agent 355 approaching his shop. He always became more aware of his slightly receding hairline and clunky glasses as she approached. He looked down at his slender form to straighten any errand clothing.

She stopped her approach to let him intercept. She saw him rearrange his clothing and looked away, grinning at the scene.

"Are you well?" he asked.

"I am, now that I see you," she said with a smile. The phrase seemed to come as a genuine opening. However, Tallmadge, for lack of knowing what to do next, gestured her into his shop without a word.

"We haven't much time," she warned as they entered, killing any chance to explore this on a personal level further. "I'm late for an engagement but wanted to bring you news. One of my lady friends was part of a celebration for the first officer of the HMS *Cerberus*. Captain Symonds was promoting his first officer to take over a sloop just captured."

Tallmadge, as did everyone, knew the *Cerberus* and her Captain John Symonds well. *Cerberus*, under her prior Captain John Chads, was the first British warship to drop anchor in Boston Harbor following the outbreak of American revolutionary hostilities. *Cerberus* brought with it not only the Parliamentary Acts, which placed countless hardships on the Americas, but also three important generals who ultimately masterminded the British war strategy—William Howe, Henry Clinton, and John Burgoyne. Local newspapers played on the origin of the name *Cerberus*—the three-headed dog with a snake's tail guarding the gates to Hell from Greek mythology—as the source of many sorrows. At the outset, the ship and her crew earnestly followed the king's orders to "lay waste, burn, and destroy" rebellious seaport towns of New England, starting with Falmouth, Maine. News of the Falmouth abuse spread, strengthening the resolve of rebellious colonists to resist. Later, the *Cerberus* even traded cannon fire with several armed Colonial vessels, including the sloop *Providence*, commanded by John Paul Jones.

"Why is this important?" asked Tallmadge, confused. The *Cerberus* had previously taken many Yankee merchantmen.

"She's moored in Connecticut in a relatively accessible anchorage as they prepare the sloop for action."

Tallmadge nodded, understanding her point. At its current anchorage, the Yankees might be able to destroy both the famous ship and the sloop. Destruction of this particular ship, with its notoriety, would give the Patriots revenge and an associated morale boost.

As a customer entered the shop, she touched his forearm and scurried from the shop.

Washington received Culper's report of the *Cerberus* almost simultaneously with news that David Bushnell's floating bomb was complete. This could prove the perfect opportunity to test the new water defense he had financed.

The water bomb initially created in the experiment at Yale College two years earlier contained a waterproof magazine housing gunpowder. More importantly, it was now equipped with a toothed wheel that rotated up and down when coming in contact with the rising and lowering hull of a vessel. This "impact mechanism" replaced the previous timed detonation device. David reasoned that a timed device was too difficult to attach and stay affixed for a later detonation. This new device, remarkably like those to be used in centuries to come, would explode on impact. If it worked, the improved floating bomb could be set afloat as a water obstacle. As such, it would be just the river protection they needed to stop the British. Now that the schooner was being refitted for the enemy, they could likewise destroy the vessel before it became fully operational and more thoroughly guarded.

David and four seamen sat in a small launch scanning the waterway. Leaning over the gunwale, he quickly looked from side to side, watching for enemy craft that could detect their approach to the *Cerberus* and the prize schooner.

"Cutter up the channel!" said a seaman. David was amazed that seamen could discern so much from a mere shadow in the darkness.

They sat silently hunched down, lest the enemy detect their presence.

The waterway now clear, they quietly made their way downriver to a position above the moored ships. Now that they were closer, David could make out a couple men in the yardarms working and two others over the side toiling away with saw and paint. "They don't waste any time, do they?" said David to nobody in particular.

"They'll have that ship fighting Yankees or frogs in no time." *Frogs* was a racial slur referring the England's archenemy, the French.

The frigate started to loom larger as they made their slow progress. Now, he could make out some sailors on deck and even the swivel guns.

"What do you make out?" David said, handing the glass to the coxswain.

"I see two small guard posts on shore. At night they'll probably have boats in the water. But there'll be room enough for us to get close and get us some redcoats." With that, a couple of men in the boat just chuckled. They had more men than they needed to scout out the enemy position, but David wanted each volunteer to see what he was getting into.

"Have you seen enough?" asked David to the sergeant of the group. He was along to check out the emplacements from a soldier's point of view.

"Yes, I'm with the coxswain. There's only light guards."

"Right, then. At the rate of their repairs, they'll have that schooner ship-shape and Bristol fashion in two days for sure. And with the in-shore squadron spread so thin, they'll not waste any time bringing that beauty into action. Is your tor-pe-do ready?" said the coxswain slowly to get it right.

"It's ready," said David, partly out of wishful thinking.

The men looked at each other. It was obvious that David was a queer bird really, with his strangeness only matched by that of his strange-looking device.

It was dark and David gave his last instructions to the small party in the boat. They all stared with some trepidation at the strange keg tied to the stern. "Go slowly with the torpedo. Don't grab the wheel with teeth at the top. Just use the line to snag the torpedo on the ship. If you can do that, it will use the current to sit next to the hull and will know when to go off," admonished David.

The men looked at David like he was from some strange place never visited by other humans. It "will know when to go off" was probably the strangest thing they had ever heard. In reality, the up and down motion of the hull would come in contact with the toothed wheel and begin an igniter inside. They held their breath as they directed the floating object toward the waiting ships.

Captain Symonds walked on the quarterdeck to see the officer of the watch and a midshipman peering over the side. As he approached, a sailor coughed. It was customary to warn officers when the captain approached.

They both straightened immediately. "Begging your pardon, Captain, but we have a line snagged on the bow."

"A line on the bow?"

"Yes, sir, a fishing line perhaps."

"Get it out of the water to make sure."

"Yes, sir."

"You and you, get that line out of the water." Two seamen scurried to the bow when one of them stopped. "Sir, two seamen on the prize are already pulling it on board."

"All right then, stand down."

As the three watched, two seamen on the prize pulled what looked like a keg out of the water. "It must be a fishing float, sir."

Just as Symonds turned away to return to his stroll, he was knocked over by the explosion. When he got to his feet, he saw that most of the prize ship was obliterated. The seamen examining the float were no more. What was left of the hulk was on fire. But he kept his wits about him.

Men started appearing from each hatch as if they were under attack.

"Drum to quarters. Get a boat in the water to look for survivors."

Gun crews manned their stations and prepared to run out, but there was no enemy in sight.

Finally the boat found one badly injured seamen floating in the water. They quickly pulled him aboard to find out what had happened. The doctor and surgeon's mate accompanied him to sickbay while Parker followed. He was breathing hard from his ordeal and still in shock, but seemed to have command of his faculties and was able to answer questions.

"What happened, man?"

"I don't know, sir. The others were examining this strange metal wheel when it started moving. It would go backwards and forwards like a clock. Then it exploded, sir." The captain touched his shoulder.

"That's fine. You rest now and let the doctor take care of you."

Symonds quickly went on deck. "Look around the ship. Are there any more kegs or lines?"

Every available lantern was hoisted. "Sir, there's still a line snagged to our bow."

"Cut it away, now!" In seconds, a seaman reported back, "It was just the remnant of the line attached to the other float."

Now that the panic was over, the first lieutenant approached the captain, "What was it, sir?"

"Those damned rebels. They're ingenious in their mischief. They made a floating bomb."

"I've never heard of such a thing, sir."

"Nor I. Clerk!"

"Yes, sir."

"Get ready to take a letter. We need to inform the admiral to watch for such hellish devices."

CHAPTER 35
ARRESTED

Townsend, alias Culper Junior, sat at the empty desk of the *New York Gazetteer* in a panic. He overhead another part-time reporter casually observe that a woman believed to be a spy for Washington had been arrested by the British. By her name and description, Townsend knew it to be so.

"How long ago?" he blurted, trying to seem controlled.

"Three days," came the response.

"Will they have a trial?" whined Townsend.

The man just looked at Townsend in confusion. Why would he ask such a thing? Everyone knew there were no trials for such an offense. They simply interrogated the accused. If they could produce no evidence or politically connected friends to vouch for their whereabouts, they would be sent to prison, or worse. The man finally responded, "No, I suppose not."

Townsend sat silent for a moment trying to compose himself under the gaze of onlookers. She should have given the British his name. She would have corroborated whatever story she wished to tell and use his position for the Tory newspaper as cover. Why wouldn't she? Then it occurred to him. She *did* feel the same about him after all. She accepted certain death in a British prison rather than place him in danger.

Townsend made an excuse and quickly rushed to the place he knew to be her residence. A scullery maid answered the door. She was obviously distraught.

"Is your mistress at home?" he inquired.

"No, sir," was all she could say. Townsend knew she could not elaborate, but he had to be sure.

"*Jersey?*" Townsend asked, not referring to New Jersey but the obvious destination for this crime, the well-known prison ship *Jersey.*

All she could do was nod her head yes, then burst into tears. It was a death sentence with no chance for a stay of execution.

Elsewhere, news of the new Yankee weapon traveled fast and David was asked to construct more floating water bombs. Between this and the water machine, ships stood at safer distances than before. Those of the in-shore squadron were more wary than ever. David was no longer viewed as a hapless inventor, but now was instrumental in the cause. In fact, one signor of the Declaration of Independence wrote a poem regarding the torpedo.

But with this notoriety, David was a hunted man. He had to be more anonymous than ever before, and he made it a point to fit into the crowd as much as he could. But time caught up with him.

David sat in Roe's tavern waiting for a contact to quietly discuss a strategy for another attack. While David quietly watched other patrons making merry, soldiers burst into the room through the front door. David jumped to his feet and instinctively looked for an exit, but almost as fast as the front door opened, soldiers burst through the back. This was David's worst nightmare come true.

"You men," yelled the fusilier. "You're under arrest for treason."

But rather than panic, David was confused. The fusilier was pointing to all of the tavern's patrons. One man's objection instantly drew a rifle butt to the head. The rest knew to be quiet.

The sergeant in charge looked at each face one by one. David tried to look calm as the fusilier stared into his face longer than the rest. Finally he moved on. After he was done, they were herded into a wagon and disappeared into the night.

Governor Trumbull sent for General Putnam as soon as he heard the word. He sat nervously in the parlor when a horse arrived with the general. His servant quickly ushered the old soldier into the room.

"So what is it that's so dammed important that you had to see me at this hour?" objected the general.

The governor just raised his hand in the direction of the unkempt man sitting in the corner.

"And who might you be, sir?"

"Begging your pardon, General. I'm Austin Row, a publican on Long Island Sound. My pub's been raided by the British."

"Well, I'm sorry about that, sir. But I'm not sure what you'd have me do."

"Oh, it's not my pub, sir, that brings me. It's that Bushnell fella."

General Putnam was now quiet and sat down. "You mean David Bushnell?"

"Yes, sir. The fusiliers got him."

He was silent for a moment. Now the governor interjected. "Tell him the rest."

"Yes, what else is there?"

"Not just him, sir. Most of the gents. They asked no names; just took them all."

The governor and general exchanged glances. That was hopeful. The British often took civilian prisoners at random, claiming that they were traitors. They'd hold them long enough to demand a prisoner exchange to get back their own officers.

"Does anyone else know that it was Bushnell they took?"

"No, sir. They haven't a clue who they got."

David sat in his cell. It was dank and foul. Human waste and vomit littered the floors and walls. David, like the rest, wasn't questioned. He realized that he'd probably been picked up in a snare to get hostages for barter. As he looked around he saw men in various states of emaciation.

The man next to David almost echoed his thoughts. "I shudder to think of the murders that have been committed here." The murders he was referring to were the deaths of neglect and starvation—not killings in the traditional sense.

David, being analytical by nature, commented, "I've heard that at least a thousand men have died here since the war began."

"More than that, laddie," interjected a man from a few feet away. By the look of his clothes and beard, he'd been here at least six months. "The lucky ones are hung. The others like that one there die more slowly."

"Hung?"

"Aye, at about half past twelve at night, they take 'em out to Barrack Street and order the people to shut their window shutters and put out their lights. The locals know that if they're caught counting the prisoners to be executed, they'll get hung themselves. That's how they does their dirty work."

"You've managed to live through it?"

"Yes. I'm safer because I'm just a shopkeeper. It's the ones that they suspect have helped the rebels that die first, followed by their own deserters. You ain't a Patriot are ye?"

David paused, trying to evade the question. "I'm just a farmer." Then he turned away for fear of being caught in the lie.

Word was quickly conveyed to Culper Junior to find the whereabouts of men arrested in Roe's tavern. It took investigating through several sources, but they were located.

In two weeks, Governor Trumbull met personally with the British negotiators. They were gentlemanly and acted like they were negotiating the sale of fine linens. He and General Putnam tried to speed up the process through every back channel they knew without raising too much suspicion. Finally, after two weeks of agonizing labor, it was almost at an end.

"So we'll exchange twelve officers for thirty Colonials plus a payment of twenty shillings?" The shillings obviously went straight into the negotiator's pocket.

"That's it, sir."

Governor Trumbull continued, "And the thirty Colonials will include the men taken on Long Island Sound." He had asked that before and was bordering on raising their suspicion, given his special interest and the fact that they were supposed to be lowly waterfront men.

"Yes. Do you have a relative in that group?"

"Of course not. My relatives would never frequent a waterfront tavern. But they're Connecticut men, popular among my constituents."

The negotiator looked unconvinced and decided to negotiate further to see what else he could get for the Colonials.

It was late at night and David was rousted from his cell. "You scum, get up. It's time to take a walk." Now David was in a panic. This was the time each night that they took men to be hanged. He looked around him and saw that each man looked terrified.

"Hurry up, we've not got all night."

One man reached for his meager coat. "You won't be needing that," the guard laughed in a sinister cackle.

David knew that this was it. As they were pushed through the dank halls with misery on every side, he thought of his brother Ezra. At least he was safe now. There was so much he wanted to do. But that obviously wasn't God's plan.

They started up Barrack Street and, as David had been told, people closed their shutters. He looked at the ground, not wanting to see the gallows. First two blocks, then four. After proceeding four blocks, David was surprised to see waiting wagons. He climbed in and sat with guards on each corner. One complained about the smell of the prisoners and held his nose. The wagons went through the streets of New York and finally into the countryside. David dared to hope they might be freed. But what if they weren't? Should they make a jump for it? If they were to be freed in exchange for other prisoners, trying to escape now would probably end in their death. But if they were on route to a mass execution, this might be their only chance. The wagons came to a stop and the men were ordered out on one side of a bridge.

David stood, praying for divine help, when a light flickered from the other side of the bridge. Twelve men in British uniforms walked across while David and the others were pushed in their direction.

"They can have these scum back anytime if you ask me," commented a British guard. "Just dung and piss, I'd say."

David fought the urge to run across the bridge and tried to compose himself. Finally they reached the other side, where Colonial soldiers were waiting. David walked to their wagons, where men were waiting with food and water.

David gulped water as if he hadn't had a drink in months. Then he felt a hand on his shoulder and jerked away in fear.

"It's all right, David."

David looked and made out the face of General Putnam. He was dressed in soldier's clothes to disguise his rank.

David couldn't speak. Instead, tears just flowed as he involuntarily cried on the general's shoulder.

After a short recovery David found himself once again in front of General Washington. As before, General Putnam and Governor Trumbull were there. He'd assumed that they wanted to talk about the torpedo and another target so he brought his latest drawing.

"Good morning, General Washington. I've made an improvement…"

This time General Putnam stopped him and waited for Washington to proceed.

"It's not what you can give us, Mr. Bushnell; it's what we have for you."

David was confused. What could they have for him?

Now it was General Putnam's turn. "Your capture gave us quite a fright, David. We realize your importance to the cause and cannot take another chance like that again."

The general turned to the governor to continue. "We feel that the best way to protect you and your weapons is to place you in the Army."

Now David was dumbfounded. General Washington continued. "And with the war now becoming less dominated by water and more a series of interior engagements, we've decided to turn you loose on land."

General Putnam reached behind a chair and brought forward a bright blue officer's coat. "David, we're creating a special unit called Sappers and Miners. We'd like you to accept a commission as a captain-lieutenant in the Continental regulars. Congress has already approved your commission."

David stood stunned. He'd somehow progressed from failure to inventor to a full-fledged officer in the Continental Army.

CHAPTER 36
SURRENDER

It was late, thought David as he gazed at the clouds moving along the shadowy horizon. They almost seemed to be slowing down to see the spectacle that was about to unfold before them. Moving his eye slowly from the sky to the treetops, he noted that most of the leaves had begun to turn various colors from orange to brown. But this was to be expected for Virginia in mid-October. The only trees still green were the pines that littered the landscape. Unfortunately, many of these trees now lay strewn about like sticks reaching in all directions. Some had fallen prey to cannonballs. Others were chopped down by battlefield engineers attempting to build defensive earthworks. That was his division, the Army Corps of Sappers and Miners.

David had seen a lot during his two years in the regulars, plus his time as an inventor before that. He looked around at the men beside him. Like him, they were ragged from head to toe. Some had pants ripped to the knees and no shoes. Most were almost skin and bone from months of deprivation. With his naturally slight build and frail appearance, David fit in easily among them.

As an officer, David had a few adornments including a blue jacket and an embroidered crest on his hat. Unlike the day it was given, it was now faded from battles and long hours of work in the forest. In dramatic contrast were the French soldiers standing opposite the Americans, with their brightly colored blue, white, and yellow uniforms. They stood gleaming against the fading sun. Many looked at the ragtag American troops with contempt. French soldiers and sailors alike saw the Colonials as amateurs who would surely have been defeated if it weren't for the French naval guns that kept the British fleet away.

But David didn't care. He looked upon them with equal contempt. He wondered how many would have joined the Army to go without pay, food, clothing, and shelter as the Americans had. Looking at their uniforms with plumes waving in the wind, he guessed that most would have just stayed home. How many had endured or seen what he'd seen?

Flanking the two rows of French and American soldiers was a pockmarked battlefield. Large mounds of earth stood behind trenches filled with pointed, protruding logs to pierce charging horses and slow-charging men. Each mound had a centerfold-like depression for the cannon to fire its nine-pounders without hindrance.

Lining the fields were spectators from Yorktown and the surrounding countryside. News that the British had finally been defeated by George Washington traveled fast. This was an occasion to celebrate. Up until now, the eight years of war had only been marked by a devastated economy and military defeats too numerous to count.

One hundred yards distant, David could see General Washington on his white charger, marking the end of the American line. The French row of soldiers was similarly marked with Fleet Commander Rochambeau on a powerful bay. Normally, they would receive the opposing general who would surrender his sword as part of a time-honored military tradition. However, in this case, General Cornwallis couldn't bring himself to face the humiliation of surrendering to Americans. Like the French, he considered the ragtag group a lesser breed. They were but civilians who left their farms and shops to shoot from behind trees and rocks instead of fighting in formal columns like a proper army should. When they did face the enemy in a column, they generally lasted only a few volleys before they broke into skirmish lines behind walls and trees.

In the distance, drummers could be heard beating the cadence for the marching soldiers in their slow advance on the Americans. Within moments, the stomp of seven thousand British infantrymen could be heard striking the beaten ground as they marched in unison. In the lead went General O'Hara, a subordinate of Cornwallis. O'Hara stood in for his commander, Cornwallis, who feigned sickness rather than face the shame of defeat.

Like the French, the British soldiers had bright, ornate uniforms signifying a professional European army. Normally they would have marched behind flag bearers with bright battle streamers. Today, however, they encased their flags as a sign of surrender. As O'Hara arrived at the head of the American line, he dismounted to present his sword to Washington, who likewise now stood on the ground.

Washington, characteristically, waived the honor. Instead, he directed O'Hara to surrender to his subordinate, General Lincoln. Only one year earlier, Lincoln had been compelled to execute a humiliating surrender to British and Loyalist troops at Charleston. It was now O'Hara's turn to lead a humiliated British Army to lay down their arms. Some were stone faced; others openly wept as they surrendered their weapons and slowly walked back to Yorktown, now prisoners of the Colonials. This defeat marked a singular change for the great army.

General Lincoln politely returned the sword just given by O'Hara, instructing instead that it be given back to Cornwallis. Before it was done, 7,000 soldiers, 2,000 sailors, 1,800 African American combatants, and 1,500 Tories (loyal to the British) turned in their arms. But at least they weren't among the 550 who died during the battle. David had survived.

CHAPTER 37
LAST REPORT

A year had passed since the surrender of Cornwallis at Yorktown. Townsend, known as Culper Junior by just a few, was settling into a life of normalcy. British Parliament had called for an end to the war in opposition to King George. Britain sent a peace envoy to Paris for negotiations with the American delegation. However, lingering questions remained. Were the British intent on peace, planning to distract the Americans for another offensive, or planning to extract serious concessions from the Continental Congress? British forces still remained in New York, and there were rumors that they planned to fortify their positions for a prolonged conflict. As a result, Washington sent word to Culper Junior asking for information from diplomatic packets shared with British officers stationed in the colonies that might contain clues to the British position. Culper Junior had given up spying and the ring disbanded. However, he accepted the assignment for closure. After his normal due diligence, Culper Junior reported:

The last packet...has indeed brought the clearest and unequivocal Proofs that the independence of America is unconditionally to be acknowledged, nor will there be any conditions insisted on for those who have joined the King's Standard.... Sir Guy himself says that he thinks it not improbable that the next Packet may bring orders for an evacuation of N. York.

A fleet is getting ready to sail for the Bay of Bundy about the first of October to transport a large number of Refugees to that Quarter.... Indeed, I never saw such general distress and dissatisfaction in my life as is painted in the countenance of every Tory at N.Y.

Culper Junior, September 19, 1782

Now it was finished. He had but bittersweet memories as his reward.

EPILOGUE

David Bushnell

After the war, David returned to his dream of creating an operable water machine and traveled to France to sell his designs. After a series of rejections, David conferred with a fellow inventor, Robert Fulton, who went on to incorporate his designs in a submarine of his own. Near the end of his disappointments, David corresponded with Thomas Jefferson, who sought information on the *Turtle* as a possible weapon against Barbary pirates. These pirates were attacking and seizing American merchant ships, launched from fortified bases in Tripoli, Tunis, and Algiers. Jefferson believed that the water machine might be able to penetrate the fortified harbors that were now unapproachable by surface warships. In response, David provided details of the *Turtle*, but elected not to pursue the idea further.

In frustration David returned to the United States, where he took up residence at the house of a fellow Yale graduate, Abraham Baldwin, in Savannah, Georgia. There he taught school and studied medicine, leading to the opening of his own medical practice in Warrenton, Georgia. He was simply known as Dr. Bush, and taught at Warrenton Academy Medical School.

Upon David's death, the residents were surprised to find his *Turtle* designs and true identity as David Bushnell.

The only recognition received for the submarine was an article entitled "General Principles and Construction of a

Submarine Vessel" by David Bushnell, October 1, 1787, printed in the *Transactions of the American Philosophical Society*, Vol IV., p. 303. Citing this and other material, his fullest exposition to being the inventor of the first operable submarine was detailed in a paper by Lieutenant Colonel Henry L. Abbott, USA, published 1881.

There are several connections that lead historians to believe that Bushnell's designs led to Robert Fulton's submarine, the *Nautilus*. Among them are two key findings. First, Dr. Bush's (David Bushnell's) Georgia roommate and former Congressman/Senator Abraham Baldwin was the brother-in-law of Yale graduate Joel Barlow, with whom Fulton lived for seven years. Barlow subsequently worked with Fulton in France, in 1797, on perfecting a self-propelled "torpedo." Barlow apparently helped Fulton to receive a commission as rear admiral in the French navy in summer 1800 (to legitimize his planned attack on the British enemy). Secondly, it is believed that David Bushnell met Robert Fulton and assisted Fulton in France during his stay.

Ezra Bushnell
Most historical accounts have Ezra Bushnell dying of camp fever. However, limited surviving records indicate that Ezra could have lived until February 16, 1786. These same records indicate that his children—Ezra, Nehemiah, Christopher Lord, David, and Nancy—were the recipients of David Bushnell's eventual estate upon David Bushnell's death in 1824.

Ezra Lee
Lee returned to his unit, where he survived the battles of Trenton, Brandywine, and Monmouth. Lee later rose to serve as a U.S. customs inspector for the new United States of America. He lived a long life and died of old age in his hometown of Lyme, Connecticut, in 1831.

Abraham Woodhull—Culper Senior
After the war, Woodhull married his cousin Mary Smith. He subsequently held several political appointments. Mary and Abraham had three children together before his remarriage after her death.

Robert Townsend—Culper Junior
After the war, Townsend ended his New York business. He remained a lifelong bachelor and ultimately shared a home with his sister until his death. It is believed that Townsend had a son, Robert Townsend Jr., by an unidentified partner. One unsubstantiated theory states that the mother was Agent 355.

Agent 355
The identity of Agent 355 has yet to be discovered. While several names have been advanced, her identity is still unknown. One theory states that she had a small role in the Culper spy ring as an associate of Culper Senior only. Other theories indicate that she served a significant role in intelligence gathering throughout the conflict. Related to this theory, it has been advanced that she had an intimate relationship with Robert Townsend, Culper Junior. She is believed to have been captured and imprisoned on the ship *Jersey*. There, it is rumored, she gave birth to a son. Some believe Robert Townsend to be the father with the boy bearing his name. She died on the prison ship.

Benjamin Tallmadge
As the war drew to a close, Tallmadge served at Washington's headquarters until the Continental Army was disbanded, where he attained the rank of lieutenant colonel. After the war, Tallmadge married Mary Floyd, daughter of Congressman and Declaration of Independence signer William Floyd. Tallmadge moved to Connecticut, where he was later elected to the United States Congress.

Caleb Brewster
After the war, Brewster married Anne Lewis and moved to Fairfield, Connecticut. After a short time as a blacksmith, Brewster joined the newly created US Revenue Cutter Service—forerunner of the US Coast Guard. Brewster went on to command the revenue cutter USRC *Active* in the War of 1812. Brewster and Anne had eight surviving children.

Austin Row
Austin Roe, owner of Roe's tavern, continued in that business, ultimately hosting George Washington during an overnight tour of Long Island in 1790. It was later determined that his brothers Nathaniel and Phillip also assisted the Culper spy ring.

Governor Jonathan Trumbull
According to legend, Trumbull became known as "Brother Jonathan" following Washington's references to that nickname in meetings. This nickname came to represent the steady and reliable people of Connecticut. Another legend states that the "johnnycake" was named after him.

General Putnam
Despite being one of the four major generals in the war, Putnam was reduced to recruiting and a minor command in Connecticut when he was felled by a paralytic stroke in 1779.

Captain Parker
Captain Parker of the HMS *Phoenix* was knighted for breaking the Yankee defenses on the Hudson River. He was later elected to Parliament.

USS *Bushnell*
The United States Navy, in recognition of Bushnell's contribution to submarine development, commissioned the submarine

tenders USS *Bushnell AS-2* and USS *Bushnell AS-15*. The USS *Bushnell AS-15* can be seen behind a moored submarine USS *Tiger* in the movie *Operation Petticoat* starring Cary Grant and Tony Curtis.

The Bushnell Brothers' Legacy

While most people think of the submarine in terms of modern warfare, it also resulted in unlocking the secrets of a new undersea world for generations to come...

"A world as strange as that of Mars," asserted William Beebe, a pioneer in undersea exploration.

BIBLIOGRAPHY

Abbot, H. L. *The Beginning of Modern Submarine Warfare* (Frank Anderson, ed.). Hamden, CT: Archon Books, 1966. (A facsimile of an 1881 pamphlet).

Bushnell, George Eleazer. *Bushnell Family Genealogy*. Richard Bingham, Oceanport, NJ, 2000.

Chant, C. *Submarines of the 20th Century*. Twickenham, England: Tiger Books Int., 1996.

Diamant, Lincoln. *Dive: The Story of David Bushnell and His Remarkable 1776 Submarine (and Torpedo)*. Fleischmanns, NY: Purple Mountain Press, 2003.

Diamant, Lincoln, and George S. Gardner. *Defending the Hudson in the American Revolution*. Fleischmanns, NY: Purple Mountain Press, 2004.

Groh, Lynn. *The Culper Spy Ring*. Philadelphia: The Westminster Press, 1969.

Johnston, Henry P. "The Record of Connecticut Men in the Military and Naval Service During the War of the Revolution 1775-1783." The Adjutant-General of Connecticut, Hartford, 1889.

Kilmeade, Brian, and Don Yaeger. *George Washington's Secret Six: The Spy Network That Saved the American Revolution.* New York: Sentinel, 2014.

Leinhard, John H. "No. 638, Bush-Bushnell." Engines of Our Ingenuity series, transcript, NPR, 1988.

Lemelson-MIT Program. "David Bushnell (1740-1826)," Inventor of the Week Archive, 2005.

PBS. "Liberty: The American Revolution." 2005.

Swanson, June. *David Bushnell and the American Turtle.* Chicago: Sequoyah Books, 2003.

Yochim, Eldred Martin. *Dar Patriot Index, Centennial Edition, Part II.* Washington: National Society of the Daughters of the American Revolution, 1990.

Made in the USA
Middletown, DE
05 July 2017